to our sons,
Jeffrey Malone Clough and Patrick Malone Clough,
with love

A HANDBOOK OF
EFFECTIVE TECHNIQUES
FOR TEACHER AIDES

A HANDBOOK OF EFFECTIVE TECHNIQUES FOR TEACHER AIDES

By

DICK B. CLOUGH, Ed.D.

*Assistant Superintendent
Marianna School District
Marianna, Arkansas*

and

BONNIE M. CLOUGH, M.Ed.

*Third Grade Teacher
Strong Elementary School
Marianna, Arkansas*

CHARLES   C   THOMAS   •   PUBLISHER
Springfield • Illinois • U.S.A.

Published and Distributed Throughout the World by
CHARLES C THOMAS ● PUBLISHER
Bannerstone House
301-327 East Lawrence Avenue, Springfield, Illinois, U.S.A.

© *1978, by* CHARLES C THOMAS ● PUBLISHER
ISBN 0-398-03809-0
Library of Congress Catalog Card Number: 78-5550

With THOMAS BOOKS *careful attention is given to all details of
manufacturing and design. It is the Publisher's desire to present books that
are satisfactory as to their physical qualities and artistic possibilities and
appropriate for their particular use.* THOMAS BOOKS *will be true to those
laws of quality that assure a good name and good will.*

Printed in the United States of America
OO-2

Library of Congress Cataloging in Publication Data
Clough, Dick B
    A handbook of effective techniques for teacher aides.

    Bibliography: p.
    Includes index.
    1. Teachers' assistants. I. Clough, Bonnie M.,
joint author. II. Title.
LB2844.1.A8C55   371.1′412   78-5550
ISBN 0-398-03809-0

INTRODUCTION

MANY educators now realize that the job of today's teacher has become virtually unmanageable. There is general agreement that teacher aides now play a vital role in making the teaching process easier to manage. Despite educators' universal endorsement of the teacher's need for assistance, however, determining how well aides will serve teachers and, ultimately, students depends upon the personal qualifications aides bring to their positions and the quality of training they receive once they begin their tasks.

Nevertheless, the presence of an aide in the classroom can potentially make a great deal of difference in the amount of individual help youngsters may receive. As a team, the teacher and her aide can bring children additional intellectual and emotional help when they need it. More depth in basic skills can be developed. Additional questions can be answered. Many errors can be minimized or even prevented. Necessary remedial work can be introduced, and basic instructional programs can be broadened.

A teacher aide can be of service in areas beyond the classroom as well as within it. Depending on where her talents and interests lie, she may assist teachers with art, music, or physical education activities. She might help with audiovisual equipment, serve as a reading tutor, work in the library, supervise children on the playground or in the cafeteria, or even assist the counselor. Above all else, she makes enlargement of the teacher's sphere of action possible.

A Handbook of Effective Techniques for Teacher Aides has been written in response to the growing and continuing need of teacher aides for a practical guide to classroom practices and procedures. It focuses on the role of the aide in the modern classroom and discusses how the aide's role is affected by the background of the children and by the organization in which she works. Emphasis has been placed on giving practical answers to the questions most often asked by teacher aides.

It is hoped that this handbook will prove valuable both for teacher aides already committed to the education profession as well as for those presently contemplating a career as an aide. It is, in fact, designed with the dual purpose of being an introductory guide as well as an in-service training tool. Also, it should further aid noncertificated personnel to come to a greater realization of the important role they play in the education of children.

D.B.C.
B.M.C.

CONTENTS

A HANDBOOK OF
EFFECTIVE TECHNIQUES
FOR TEACHER AIDES

CHAPTER 1

WHAT IS A TEACHER AIDE?

USING auxiliary personnel to supplement the teacher's work in the classroom is not a new idea. In the traditional one-room schoolhouse of bygone days, older children listened as younger pupils recited a memorized assignment or read pages from their primer. Volunteers came to assist in the schools during the war years when certified professions were at a premium. As early as 1952, Bay City, Michigan, launched a program to use teacher aides; the idea soon spread to other communities in adjoining states. The practice of using teacher aides in school systems has accelerated enormously during the past decade and continues to grow today.

While the concept of teacher aides is not new, the nature of the aide's role is such that it still remains difficult to define terms clearly and concisely with the assurance that the various terms have the same meaning for all who use them. Obviously, the role of an aide varies from school to school and even from classroom to classroom within the same school. How a teacher aide is used depends primarily upon the unique needs of the community, the school, and the students. However, most educators agree that teacher aides are individuals who work directly under the supervision of certificated personnel and perform duties that are of a routine, noninstructional, or semi-instructional nature. Such individuals have a supportive role and should not in any case supplant the certificated personnel within the school district.

Teacher aides come from diverse backgrounds — they may be high school students or senior citizens, inner-city or suburban housewives, high school dropouts or college graduates, or even retired persons. In addition, they may have a variety of titles — school aide, teacher assistant, educational associate, community aide, library assistant, instructional aide, clerical assistant, classroom aide, or auxiliary worker. Nevertheless, each teacher aide brings to her job a unique personality, a varied collection of skills and abilities, and a rich background of experiences that distinguishes her from all other teacher aides and staff members.

ROLE OF THE TEACHER AIDE

As each school strives to adjust its methods of instruction to meet the needs of all students, the professional staff should be released from many routine tasks that can be easily performed by aides. Educational research has revealed that about one third of the time of the professional teacher's time is spent on instruction, while the other two thirds of her time is spent on routine nonteaching tasks. An aide can be successfully employed to perform many of these routine tasks and to assist the teacher in many other appropriate duties.

Frequently, a distinction is made between instructional and noninstructional aides, the primary difference being whether or not the aide has direct and sustained contact with children in the classroom. The noninstructional aide may perform housekeeping, clerical, material preparation, or community-oriented tasks almost exclusively. The instructional support aide, on the other hand, usually works directly with youngsters under the supervision of a classroom teacher. Her duties may, however, also include some clerical, housekeeping, or technically oriented tasks.

A recent survey by the NEA Research Division has given the following breakdown as to types of assistance provided by aides at the elementary and secondary levels.

Job Responsibility	Total (%)	Elementary (%)	Secondary (%)
Clerical assistance	77.8	73.0	85.9
Assistance with nonclassroom duties	18.4	25.7	7.1
Assistance with large group instruction	15.9	16.3	15.2
Assistance with small group instruction	13.7	18.5	5.1

Job Responsibility	Total (%)	Elementary (%)	Secondary (%)
Preparation and use of instructional resources	13.4	15.7	9.1
Assistance with classroom environment	8.6	10.7	5.1
Other	0.7	1.1	0.0

Depending in large measure upon her basic skills and educational background, there is a wide range of useful activities that a teacher aide can perform. Some aides, for instance, who are either college graduates or who have a considerable amount of college course work, can handle many instructional duties. Even though most aides have only a high school education, they bring to their job a variety of skills useful to both children and teachers. For example, their assistance may involve such a simple but essential task as giving an upset child understanding and comfort when the teacher lacks the time to do so.

Obviously, the introduction of a teacher aide in a classroom creates a more supportive and encouraging environment for learning. All learning experiences require a certain degree of adult direction and supervision. An effective teacher aide can bring to the classroom the needed support to facilitate student academic and social growth.

When teacher aides are sensitive to the nature of child growth and development, they can play a significant role as a second adult within the classroom. Moreover, they can take a positive, active part in instructional interaction with individual students, small groups, or even, on occasion, with the entire class.

QUALIFICATIONS

There are some attributes a teacher aide must have that are not taught in either pre- or in-service training. These qualities are the characteristics that make up the teacher aide as a person. You should be sure that you possess these traits before you begin to make preparation for an aide position.

Importance of Physical Health

Being a teacher aide is hard work. If you have frequent head-aches, recurring colds, tired spells, or other chronic conditions that reduce vitality, you should not try to be a teacher aide. Also, children should not be in contact with individuals who have frequent infections; in fact, in most states, a teacher or aide is not allowed to be with students unless she shows satisfactory evidence of being free of contagious diseases.

It would be a waste of time and effort for you to be trained as a teacher aide if it is doubtful you could pass the necessary physical examination for employment. The teacher aide must have excellent health — not just enough vitality to get by, but an abundance of energy.

Importance of Mental Health

Of equal importance with good physical health is good mental health. Teacher aides sometimes fail because of a lack of emotional stability. An aide must face situations every day that demand mental balance and good emotional stability. How you meet such situations often determines your success or failure. Administrators report that more teacher aides fail because of poor mental health than because of poor physical health. Aides are in an important position every minute of the school day. Their reactions to problem situations are of the greatest importance.

A love of children is an important prerequisite for the well-adjusted teacher aide. No one should attempt to be an aide who does not get great satisfaction out of associations with children. Patience and self-control are essential virtues when working with children. Displaying enthusiasm for the work to be accomplished helps develop a good working environment within the school. The aide who is cheerful, good-natured, and seldom upset has a much greater chance of success than the emotionally unstable or the mentally troubled person. This person has no business working with children and can expect little success.

Importance of Personality

Satisfactory matching of an individual's unique personality to his job requirements is closely related to his physical and mental health. This consideration is extremely important in the work of a teacher aide. Some personalities are not easily adapted to working with youngsters. Some individuals who make good secretaries would not make good aides; some who are successful store clerks would not succeed as teacher aides; others might be excellent bookkeepers but would make poor aides. Different vocations require different kinds of personalities. It is important to note that not all aide positions require the same type of personality. The personality necessary for a successful kindergarten aide might be very different from that required of a library assistant at the high school level.

Do not make the mistake of thinking that you must be an extrovert to be a successful teacher aide. However, it would be wise to discuss this matter with a teacher, administrator, or someone else who knows you well and also knows the kind of personality that is best suited to being a teacher aide.

Importance of Moral Character

Everyone agrees that an individual who works closely with children should be of good moral character. A teacher aide deals with children the entire day. Therefore, many of the habits that the children may be expected to imitate and develop are likely to be habits that are practiced by teacher aides. In order to be a good example, an aide should avoid displaying characteristics usually associated with an immoral individual. Some children come from homes that are on a low moral plane, and most of their socially desirable habits must be fostered by the school and its staff. The teacher aide carries a great responsibility.

Importance of Adequate Intelligence

The fact that an individual has graduated from high school

should be some evidence that she has the necessary general intelligence to become a teacher aide. If her high school record is above average, that also is a good indication. Although the exact duties an aide is expected to perform have a direct bearing on the required intelligence, almost every position requires the ability to read and write satisfactorily. In addition, aides must have sufficient resourcefulness to conduct activities indirectly related to the teaching process.

RECRUITMENT

There are a variety of methods by which teacher aides are recruited. Differences in methods are usually the result of the size and location of the school district as well as the particular job requirements. Although recruitment may take the form of advertisements in the local newspaper, more often than not, the information about the availability of teacher aide openings is spread by word-of-mouth. However, some districts choose to recruit prospective aides by contact with organizations within the community. Regardless of the method used to announce the availability of aide positions, the first step toward employment is the completion of a written application form.

Application Form

Usually, prospective teacher aides are required to complete a formal written application prior to either a job interview or employment. In most cases, the application form is your first official introduction to school personnel. Every effort should be made to complete the form as accurately and as neatly as possible. First impressions often mean the difference between success and failure in obtaining employment.

The application form itself serves as both a criterion for selection and a source of personal information about the applicant. You can expect the form to include the usual informational data, such as name, address, age, Social Security number, education and training, and marital status, etc. Sometimes a statement describing your personal philosophy and beliefs in regard to education is requested. If either personal or professional references are required, it is wise to ask permission from the individuals involved prior to submitting their names. Sometimes letters of recommendation may also be necessary. Select people who really know you well and can make an honest evaluation of your future performance. Your clergyman, family physician, or a close friend can serve as a dependable personal reference. Professional references should always include your most recent employer, in addition to individuals who are acquainted with your past work record. Relatives should never be included as either personal or professional references.

A sample application form is included for your study. An examination of its contents should aid you in completing future application forms. Be prepared to discuss anything that you have stated on the application form.

The Interview

The interview is the most common method used by school districts to appraise applicants' desirability for the position of teacher aide. The session may be conducted by the district personnel department, a school principal, a special aide-program consultant, a teacher, or by a combination of these. In some cases, applicants may be interviewed in a group so that they will feel more at ease. The interviewer may question you to gain insight regarding such matters as language competence, previous work experience, and special talents. The interviewer may also ask about your willingness to work with mentally or physically handicapped children or inquire about your feelings regarding being assigned to a school other than the one nearest your home.

While it is only natural to experience some anxiety during a job interview, the following suggestions may prove helpful in preparation for your next job interview:

1. Be on time for the interview.
2. Come alone; if you have children, hire a babysitter.
3. Dress neatly and appropriately.
4. Don't criticize past employers.
5. Answer questions directly and fully, but don't ramble on

TEACHER AIDE APPLICATION FORM

Name_____ Date_____

Present Address_____ Phone_____

Permanent Address_____ Phone_____

Date of Birth_____ Place of Birth_____

General Health_____ Height_____ Weight_____

Marital Status: Single_____ Married_____ Divorced_____ Widowed_____

Number of Children_____ Ages_____

Education:

High School and/or College	Degree	Year	Major
_____	_____	_____	_____
_____	_____	_____	_____
_____	_____	_____	_____

Work Experience (Last position listed first)

Firm	Position	Dates	Reason for Leaving
_____	_____	_____	_____
_____	_____	_____	_____
_____	_____	_____	_____
_____	_____	_____	_____

In what capacities have you previously worked with children?

_____

_____

Why do you feel you would like to become a teacher aide?

_____

_____

Do you play a musical instrument?_____ If so, what?_____

References:

Name	Position & Firm	Address
_____	_____	_____
_____	_____	_____
_____	_____	_____

aimlessly.

6. Be sure to mention past work experience that provided helpful training for working as a teacher aide.
7. Demonstrate a sincere interest in the job of being a teacher aide.
8. If you have special talents in music, art, stitchery, or sports, be sure to mention them.
9. Don't do all the talking. Listen to what the interviewer has to say.
10. When the interview is over, thank the interviewer for considering your application.

Selection

The selection process usually begins in the school district's central office. More often than not, aides are selected by the same procedure used to select other noncertificated personnel. After the initial interview is over, you will probably be referred to a school principal, who will reexamine your application form and possibly conduct a second interview. If you are to work in a team teaching situation, the team leader may also be involved in the initial selection process.

In accepting initial employment with a school, the beginning aide should make certain that she understands the conditions of her employment. Pertinent points regarding various aspects of the position should be clarified before signing a contract. Ask, for instance, if the position is permanent or temporary, what the nature of the assignment will be, what the salary is and what method of payment is offered, and whether or not there are opportunities for advancement. Even if a written contract is not offered, the conditions of employment should be clearly understood by the aide, so that any disputes that may arise can be settled on the basis of the initial agreement.

CERTIFICATION

It is the general practice for personnel in health, education, and welfare enterprises to be certified or licensed. Individuals working in these vital areas are expected to have a level of proficiency and academic preparation in keeping with the important duties they will be called upon to perform. For example, the minimum preparation for the classroom teacher has been set as the baccalaureate degree (four-year degree). Most educational administrators are required to obtain a master's degree prior to certification.

At the present time, no specific certification requirements have been clearly established nationwide for auxiliary personnel. However, some states have adopted guidelines or minimum standards for teacher aides. Others have begun the practice of certifying all nonteaching personnel in their schools. Illinois, for instance, makes a distinction for certification purposes between instructional and the noninstructional aides. The instructional aide must have thirty hours of college credit and must perform her duties under the direct supervision of a certificated teacher. Aides working in noninstructional capacities have no minimum requirements.

Even though most states have not provided for teacher aide certification, the various state departments of education have developed guidelines for the employment of auxiliary personnel. Most of them urge the establishment of personnel policies, standards, and procedures for selecting and employing teacher aides at the local level. In addition, they recommend that certificated personnel periodically review and revise selection procedures for noncertificated personnel.

While the prospective aide should become familiar with her own local and state requirements for employment and/or certification, most school districts have established similar qualifications:

- Eighteen years of age or over
- United States citizen
- High school diploma or its equivalent
- Good command of the English language
- Suitable personal qualities
- Character references and health requirements

LEGAL CONSIDERATIONS

In any consideration of the utilization of teacher aides in the classroom, the question of legal authority and liability becomes particularly important. All states have certification laws that require individuals to meet certain minimal qualifications before they are eligible to become teachers in the schools. Therefore, unless there are state statutes that cover teacher aides, an aide is not authorized to substitute for a certificated teacher or to become involved in disciplining children.

The courts have ruled that school personnel are duty-bound to exercise the same care a parent using ordinary prudence would exercise under comparable circumstances. The obligation to be reasonably cautious exists in the classroom as well as on the playground. If a child is injured as a direct result of an individual's failure to show care, that individual is personally liable. He or she cannot escape by trying to shift the legal burden to his or her school district.

Generally speaking, courts hold that lack of proper supervision is one circumstance that makes school employees personally liable for student injury. Increasingly, there seems to be a greater inclination for juries to return verdicts for substantial amounts of money. The underlying principle seems to be that "a teacher or other school employee may be held personally liable for injuries, directly or indirectly sustained by a child under the individual's care, that result from that person's negligence or failure in the line of duty."

When teacher aides are assigned tasks involving the supervision of students, they can be placed in a position of potential liability for pupil injury unless specific policies give the aide the same protection afforded student teachers and regular teachers. However, since most of the duties assigned aides are carried out under the direct supervision of a classroom teacher or a team of teachers, the question of liability should not present a problem.

When working directly with students, teacher aides are well advised to make certain that they know the scope of their duties and the limit of their responsibilities. It would be advisable, also, for teacher aides to be provided instruction on how to deal with such matters as student injury, misbehavior by children, and responsibilities children may or may not assume. If for no other reason than for their own protection, aides should have a thorough knowledge of their own rights, limitations of authority, and responsibilities. With a minimum of foresight and a generous supply of common sense, teacher aides can prevent legal problems from arising.

ETHICAL CONCERNS

You are probably aware that most professions have a code of ethics that defines and describes acceptable practices for their members. As professionals, educators adhere to such a code of conduct. Teachers are expected to conduct their lives in an ethical manner. Relationships with children, parents, and others within the community must have a strong ethical basis. A strong code of ethics must match the major doctrines of the professional. By constantly referring to the code and making one's actions adhere to the code, teachers operate as professionals in the truest sense of the word.

The ethical code of the teacher aide should not differ significantly from that of the professional teacher. Aides must have an underlying belief in a deep sense of moral justice and must show respect for ethical considerations. Operating without basic ideals, teachers and aides will surely experience difficulty in adapting to the everyday problem situations that inevitably arise. Following the ethics of your own personal philosophy as well as the ethics of the teaching professional provides proper guidance in your interactions with children and adults. A well-integrated and consistent set of values encourages all members of the school staff to work together in harmony.

In fulfilling her obligations to students, parents, and the teaching profession itself, the aide shall —

- Make reasonable effort to protect the students from conditions that may prove harmful to the learning process or to health and safety.

- Conduct professional activities in such a manner as to avoid exposing the student to unnecessary embarrassment or disparagement.
- Not use professional relationships with students for private advantage.
- Hold in confidence information that has been obtained in the course of professional services.
- Not knowingly distort or misrepresent facts concerning educational matters in direct or indirect public expressions.
- Accept no gifts or favors that might impair or appear to impair professional judgment, nor offer any favor, service, or object of value to obtain special advantage.
- Award just and equitable treatment to all members of the teaching profession in the exercise of their professional rights and responsibilities.

PROFESSIONAL RELATIONSHIPS

Aides find that most teachers welcome the addition of a teacher aide to the staff. They view aides as partners in the task of educating children. However, a minority of classroom teachers still resent or fear teacher aides. The source of this fear and resentment can usually be found in past patterns of teacher assignments. Most teachers have spent their entire career teaching alone in a self-contained classroom. They have not had to share their students or classrooms with anyone else, nor have they had to work closely with another adult. When faced with using a teacher aide, these teachers may become insecure and resent the person whom they consider to be the intruder in their classroom.

Teachers' fear and resentment must be dispelled if children are to enjoy the full benefits of having a teacher aide in the classroom. An effective way to overcome this fear is to make aides available only to those teachers who recognize their value and ask for them. If these teachers make good use of aides, other teachers most certainly will follow suit, and the final result is that the school's program is significantly improved.

Always remember that as a teacher aide you have the responsibility to show other staff members the respect and consideration due professional personnel. As a member of the educational team, you must observe the confidential nature of such relationships. For instance, an aide learns a great deal of confidential information about the children she works with; therefore, it is important for her not to discuss the children with whom she works, except with the professional staff. At no time should an aide commit an act or make any statement that undermines the teacher's position of leadership or destroys the teacher-student relationship.

Furthermore, the teacher aide should never interfere with the responsibility of the teacher in conferences with parents. Under certain circumstances where the teacher feels that the aide can be of assistance, she may be invited to participate in the teacher-parent conference. Otherwise, she must refrain from becoming involved in the teacher's dealings with parents and the community in general.

Although minor personality conflicts are bound to occur in any organization, conflicts between teachers and aides can have an adverse affect on children's educational opportunities. In any serious or prolonged conflict, the teacher aide almost always has to be transferred to another classroom. However, every effort should be made by both the aide and the teacher to resolve the differences and to reestablish a successful working relationship. The education of children is too serious an enterprise to let personal pride stand in the way of good staff relationships.

As a teacher aide, you are expected to follow the school district's procedures and practices in the same manner as the other staff members. Special consideration should be given to the following practices:

1. Teacher aides should keep confidential any personal information learned about students or teachers and should refrain from making unprofessional comments about a student or teacher.
2. Teacher aides should deal justly and impartially with stu-

dents, regardless of their economic, social, racial, or religious background.

3. Teacher aides should recognize the educational differences of children and should seek to meet their individual needs.
4. Teacher aides should conduct themselves in a responsible manner in the development and implementation of school policies.
5. Teacher aides should be aware of the necessity and importance of respecting the dignity of all persons.
6. Teacher aides should maintain professional and ethical conduct as representatives of the school district.

SUMMARY

Social, educational, and economic factors have led to a sharp increase in the number of teacher aides employed in schools during the past decade. While aides are not intended to replace teachers, they can provide needed support and assistance within the regular classroom. This contribution, at the outset, permits teachers to have more time to assess individual student needs and, ultimately, improves the quality of classroom instruction.

As a teacher aide, your primary function and responsibility is to increase the effectiveness of the teacher in the classroom. You can expect to be called upon to do a variety of tasks to assist teachers with the preparation, presentation, and culmination of classroom activities. However, the kind and quality of tasks you are asked to perform depend upon your own competency.

CHAPTER 2

WORKING WITH THE CLASSROOM TEACHER

As educational practices continuously change, the modern classroom is becoming more and more a creative workshop where youngsters learn by doing. Today's students learn through open discussion, through critical thinking, and at their individual paces. Where do you as an aide fit into the classroom scheme? You can make it possible for teachers to have time to confer about lesson plans and students' learning problems. You can help teachers by setting up a science experiment, assisting with a music lesson, constructing a bulletin board, acting out a story, or teaching a game. Thus, you become a vital assistant to the classroom teacher, an extra set of hands, and a friend and counselor to students. You give the teacher flexibility, permitting her to take the time to work with a special reading group, to teach a new concept to the class, or to solve disagreements between students.

However, if teacher aides are to realize their full effectiveness as classroom assistants, they must develop the necessary essential skills. Too often, aides are looked upon as nothing more than clerical assistants and are given little opportunity to become involved in instructional activities. Their work has been limited to grading student papers, operating audiovisual equipment, taking the lunch count, and keeping records. While all of these tasks are essential, it is clear that classroom aides are not being used to the best advantage in the teaching-learning process.

The teacher aide's position must be justified primarily in terms of the benefits it brings to students. The only truly proper utilization of the aide is in a classroom assignment where she works under the direct guidance and supervision of a teacher. Within the classroom, an aide's primary concern should be with the students' educational and social development. Using an aide for nothing more than duplicating materials or correcting papers defeats the major purpose of the aide's position. A teacher aide's function should differ only in degree and not in substance from that of the regular teacher.

MEETING YOUR CO-WORKERS

Many new teacher aides are apprehensive about joining a school staff for the first time and meeting the established faculty. Naturally, the returning staff members are already acquainted with each other and with the policies and procedures that govern their work. Without meaning to, they may seem to form an ingroup that arouses concern in a new teacher aide. Some of this apprehension is caused by such fears as making a poor first impression, saying the wrong thing at the wrong time, or forgetting staff members' names. If these normal, but common, fears make you feel insecure, it might be well to keep in mind the following:

1. The best way to make a good impression is to try to put the other person at ease. Just remember that he or she doesn't know what to expect either. Often you can put another person at ease by simply smiling, by dressing conservatively, or by asking for help and advice. If you show a genuine liking for another person, usually that person will return the same friendliness.

2. When you are new in a group, one of the best ways to say the right thing at the right time is to listen to the other people talk and then ask intelligent questions. Avoid beginning a new relationship with a controversial topic of conversation. Wait until you get to know the other person well enough to speak frankly with him. Do not participate in "gripe sessions" early in the year (if ever). Listen if you must, but don't join in. More than likely, you will come to regret anything you say rashly.

3. People who are good at remembering names usually work at it. They develop memory techniques that help fix names in their minds. Use the new person's name several times during the initial conversation. It is helpful to examine the individual you are meeting for any characteristics that can serve as an aid

in remembering the person's name. Don't panic if you forget someone's name. Most people realize that newcomers have many more names to learn than the returning staff members. If you forget someone's name, even the name of the new teacher you are working with, apologize with a smile, and ask for it again.

4. Be sure to introduce yourself to the custodians, secretaries, and cafeteria employees. They will appreciate your giving them the opportunity to discuss their work with you and to suggest ways in which they can work efficiently and effectively with you. They all play an important role in the education of children.

If you are a returning teacher aide, do all you can to minimize the problems outlined above. Remember to mention your name the first three or four times you meet a new staff member. It is also considerate to introduce them to the other staff members, include them in your conversations, and even to take them to coffee during the orientation workshop. In short, think about the time when you were new to the school, and do what you hoped others would do for you to make you feel accepted.

DEVELOPING THE ART OF COOPERATING

Teacher aides are more frequently dismissed from their positions for failing to get along with their fellow workers than for not possessing the required job skills. At times, people are inclined to overestimate their own personal significance and their position's importance in relationship to the total program of the institution they serve. Aides may become frustrated when other staff members see things differently.

An aide may become irritated at a teacher who gives her something to duplicate five minutes before the end of the school day. The teacher cannot understand the aide's ire because, "After all, that's what she's being paid to do. Without materials to duplicate, she would be out of a job." The aide feels that the teacher could be more considerate in scheduling times for duplicating materials. If the aide and her teacher harbor ill feelings toward each other over such a situation, it is possible that their continuing relationship as cooperative co-workers will rapidly deteriorate and have a detrimental effect on the children involved.

Simply put, the task of the school is to educate children. Through their specific assignments, all staff members share in this responsibility. Since teacher aides make up a sizeable block of workers in most schools, they bear a large responsibility for helping to insure a cooperative atmosphere among the school's staff.

Someone has to be responsible for coordinating classroom activities and for making decisions that are best made by one person. When you accept an assignment to be an aide in a school, you also accept the leadership of the teachers to whom you will be assigned. This does not mean that the teacher is infallible; rather, it means that you agree to work with her in the execution of your common responsibilities. You are obligated to accept decisions that teachers are required to make, just as they are obligated to back you up on classroom and playground decisions you are required to make.

You have to learn to get along with your classroom teacher if you are going to work together as a team in carrying out the goals of the school. Discuss all differences of opinion on a professional level, and have a friendly cup of coffee together after the discussion is finished, even if you agree to disagree." Vigorously chase away feelings of dislike, jealousy, and unhealthy competition. A good faculty is made up of many individuals, each contributing what is uniquely his or hers. Don't try to remake your colleagues to fit your own image of what a teacher or aide should be. Share with them the ideas and talents that you have, and draw from them what they have to offer.

Go out of your way to be friendly and helpful to new staff members. Don't fill them in on all the unpleasant aspects of work in your school. Accent that which is good and challenging so that their first days and weeks will be exciting. If you are a new aide yourself, go out of your way to be friendly and approachable to more experienced aides on the staff. Don't hesitate to ask them for help and advice. Most people are flattered when others ask them for help.

Get in the habit of commending special effort on the part of co-workers with memos of thanks directed to the individual or individuals responsible. Anyone can say "Thanks," but it takes more effort to write it down. Extra effort on your part for a little extra effort on their part seems a fair exchange.

Here are some questions that may help you determine whether or not you have established that needed rapport with your fellow co-workers:

1. Do I try to develop a friendly attitude toward all of my co-workers?
2. Do I make myself helpful by offering my services to the teacher when there is an obvious need for help?
3. Do I observe closely the techniques used by the teacher and follow them when I am working with the class?
4. Do I accept criticism and suggestions without becoming emotionally upset?
5. Do I follow the directions of the classroom teacher?
6. Do I realize that my primary purpose for being in the classroom is to assist the teacher so that children might progress more rapidly?
7. Do I avoid criticism of the teacher, other aides, and the school?

FINDING OUT ABOUT THE TEACHER'S EXPECTATIONS

Open and effective communication is of the utmost importance in the teacher-aide relationship. Most classroom problems can be avoided if effective communication channels are kept open between the classroom teacher and the teacher aide. Early in your working relationship, you should ask the teacher with whom you are working to outline her expectations of your role. She probably knows in her own mind exactly what is expected, but you will never know unless she tells you. Open communication removes much of the guesswork and uncertainty commonly associated with being a teacher aide.

One valuable tool for learning your teacher's expectations of your role is the teacher-aide conference. This session can play a

---

FOR YOU TO FIND OUT

1. Your special and regular duties
2. Which records you are responsible for keeping
3. Special services available to the classroom and the school in which you work
4. Schedules you are responsible for following
5. Emergency provisions that apply to your situation
6. Where and when children in your classroom play
7. Location of special rooms and facilities in your school
8. Priorities on your time
9. The most important playground regulations
10. Lunch-time activities for which you are responsible
11. Location of supplies and how they are kept and obtained
12. Location of equipment which is available and procedures for obtaining it
13. The line of communication and authority you are to follow
14. Location of pupil records available to you
15. How your time is divided if you are responsible for working with more than one teacher
16. To whom you should direct questions concerning school policy
17. What is expected of you in terms of student discipline
18. What course you should follow if you feel that you do not have enough to do
19. What course you should follow if you feel that you have too much to do
20. How your teacher views the teacher-aide relationship

---

vital role in encouraging professional growth experiences in both parties. An initial conference should be held early in the aide's work experience. An early conference allows you time to intelligently modify incorrect behavior. Too often, teachers indicate deficiencies only on the final written evaluation — after it is too late. Obviously, it is wise to communciate early and often.

You will make mistakes from time to time just as teachers do.

It is important that you discuss areas in which you need improvement soon after deficiencies become apparent. Not only should you discuss these mistakes, but, with your teacher, you should agree on strategies to correct the situation. Failure to develop a well-conceived plan of attack to conquer problems has lead to the dismissal of many aides.

What meaningful topics could be discussed during these conferences? It is a simple matter for both you and your teacher to write down questions and concerns as they arise. In addition, such conferences can also be used to review your progress, to clear up uncertainties, and to plan classroom strategies in working with your students.

Finally, the rapport you develop with your teacher determines to a great extent the success of your conference. In order to build rapport, you both need to show sensitivity, respect, warmth, and sincerity in your dealings with each other. As you strive to improve your rapport and establish worthwhile conference topics, it may prove helpful to spend some time evaluating your work habits.

In order to have good teacher-aide relationships, there should be mutual respect and good will. Therefore, teacher aides should —

1. Read and observe the rules of the school to which they are assigned.
2. Be aware that various teachers may have different teaching styles yet work successfully with children in their own ways. Be aware that the presence of a new adult in the classroom may be disturbing or distracting to the children at first; therefore, be patient when providing help.
3. Adhere to the teacher's standard of behavior for her children and support her in disciplinary matters.
4. Remember to be loyal to teachers, students, and school administrators at all times. Refrain from discussing personalities with other staff members.
5. Discuss questions, problems, or suggestions with the appropriate designated personnel in the school.

ACCEPTING CONSTRUCTIVE CRITICISM

It has been said that one of the problems with criticism is that "any fool can engage in it, and most fools do." Offering constructive criticism without arousing resentment is considered a fine art in human relations. The problem is that everyone likes to protect his or her own ego, or self. Pride causes most people to find it difficult to accept even constructive criticism with grace.

Most experienced supervisors have found that criticism is most effective when it is done in a relaxed manner. No one likes to be criticized sarcastically or severely. Such criticism does more harm than good. Criticism should not be administered if its purpose is to show anger, to punish, or to create unhappiness. The sole purpose of criticism should be to help the individual to understand what specific behavior can be improved and to inspire him or her to do better.

However, all of us need constructive criticism from time to time. When that time comes and you are confronted with criticism, do not become angry, sarcastic, or discourteous to your supervisor. Recognize that there is a place for legitimate differences of opinion in most actions that people undertake. You will find that it is much easier to accept criticism if you make it a practice to conduct self-evaluations on your own performance on a continuing basis. Often, the teacher's suggestions for improvement will closely parallel your own self-criticism.

Most teacher aides find that effective classroom performance lessens the need for constructive criticism. You may find it useful to continually reevaluate your own performance by answering the following questions for yourself:

1. Do I make sufficient plans for the activities to which I have been assigned — not merely a hit-or-miss effort just to "do something?"
2. Do I observe closely in order to know children's preferences, likes, dislikes, enthusiasms, and aversions, etc.?
3. Do I really listen to what the children have to say?
4. Do I learn as much about each student as quickly as

possible?

5. Do I lend personal assistance to students whenever possible?
6. Do I praise each student's efforts and successes?
7. Do I consult often with the teacher on how I can assist her?
8. Am I patient in dealing with students?
9. Am I acquainted with emergency procedures?
10. Have I learned the routine of the school day?
11. Do I evaluate myself at intervals during the school year?

THE TEACHER'S ROLE

Before you can fully understand your own role as a teacher aide, you must have a clear picture of the teacher's role in the classroom. Basically, the teacher's task is to plan and select instructional materials and methods, to organize and manage the classroom, and to evaluate student progress. This involves working with students, fellow teachers, administrators, parents, and community members. The teacher must also plan lessons, develop instructional materials, help students with numerous personal problems, grade homework and tests, and complete reports. Patience, dedication, and fortitude are qualities that the classroom teacher must have in abundance.

Obviously, the concept of a teacher whose duties are limited only to "hearing lessons," "holding class," and "keeping discipline," is far too limited. Like the school system of which she is the keystone, the teacher has additional relationships that transcend the bounds of her classroom and school building. As a member of the school community who provides a link with the larger community, her relationships are shared with many others, and she functions best as part of a cooperative community effort.

In the classroom, you will learn that the primary purpose of the teaching process is to make certain desirable changes in the lives of children, changes involving growth and development in such attributes as knowledge, habits, skills, ideals, attitudes, and appreciation. The teacher, as the director of learning, is successful only when she helps to bring about these desirable changes. If growth is not encouraged and if the changes are not desirable, then the teaching process has failed.

Someone has said, "Education is worth precisely the difference it makes in the activities of the individual being educated." Some of these differences can be measured and evaluated; however, some of the most important ones cannot. It is easy enough to measure the number of words a child can spell or his accuracy in adding or subtracting. It is not so easy to measure a child's growth in the development of such values as honesty, fair-mindedness, courtesy, or ideals.

Once you are in the classroom, you may also find that teachers are better educated today than ever before. They know better than teachers ever have how to teach effectively. However, greater demands upon their time and changing educational technology are preventing many of them from doing the kind of job they have been trained to do. Teachers, therefore, very often feel guilty about the kind of job they are able to do in the classroom. For these and similar reasons, it is easy to conclude that teachers are greatly in need of assistance in carrying out the teaching-learning process. Therefore, the teacher aide who works with the teacher can prove to be a valuable asset by making the teacher's job more manageable and by helping her to perform tasks more effectively. Your duties might include: (1) helping the teacher plan, organize, and present activities and locate resources; (2) tutoring individual students or instructing small groups; (3) lending needed support in maintaining classroom discipline; and (4) assisting her with routine tasks. The nature of the work you perform in the classroom depends in large measure upon the teacher's and your own capabilities and the rapport you develop with each other.

LEARNING TO PLAN

Planning in any successful endeavor is important. A minister must have a sermon outline, an engineer needs his blueprints, a lawyer must plan his briefs, and a teacher must prepare her daily lessons. It is unlikely that you would want to be the patient of a doctor who operated by guessing, or that you would want to have a house built by a contractor who works without a blueprint. While the beginning teacher aide has a greater need for detailed written plans than does an experienced aide, there is no justification for anyone being involved in classroom learning activities without the benefit of some prior planning. The type of daily planning you are required to do is usually dependent upon:

1. The required policy used in your school district
2. The philosophy and values held by your classroom teacher
3. The accepted standard of practice in your school
4. The nature of the student experiences in which you will be involved

As a new teacher aide, you will soon learn that the time spent in the classroom can be constructive only if the teacher and you have planned worthwhile activities. Unfortunately, many teachers make the mistake of depending too much on "playing it by ear." They depend on too much personal operation and too little constructive planning. If you are going to be able to do the job you were hired to do, then a great deal of planning is required. This means planning not only by the classroom teacher, but planning on your part as well.

The actual writing of teacher aide plans and the amount of detail they should contain depends upon your experience with effective planning and the type of instructional situation in which you are involved. Nevertheless, whether you are tutoring a student, listening to children read, or showing a film, a well-developed instructional plan is a necessity. Your plan should contain six basic components: (1) basic objectives, (2) content, (3) procedures, (4) instructional activities, (5) equipment and materials, and (6) evaluation methods.

Basic Objectives

It is important that objectives be formulated as a first step in any instructional activity. The objectives identify what is to be learned by the student and give directions on how the learning is to be accomplished. Further, they explain in detail what it is that the student will be able to do at the conclusion of instruction. Objectives help to insure that instructional activities are result oriented.

The functions of an objective can best be shown by presenting the basic elements essential to a well-written objective:

1. *Behavior:* A description of the expected final behavior that can be observed by at least two different observers.
2. *Conditions:* A statement of the conditions under which the behavior is to be observed.
3. *Criteria:* A statement of the criteria of acceptable performance, including the means by which the observer will be able to measure performance.

Example: When administered a written test, the student will be able to answer nine out of ten assigned division problems correctly.

Content

The content selected in any instructional activity should reflect the stated objectives. The way the content is selected and arranged for study should be based upon the knowledge of how students learn best. The amount of content to be included and in what depth the content is to be studied is always determined by the classroom teacher, never by the aide alone. However, once the initial content is selected, aides are usually permitted to make additional minor decisions in regard to the scope and sequence of content as it relates to the activities undertaken.

Procedures

The third part of an instructional plan involves the procedures the teacher and aide follow in carrying out the instructional process. In essence, procedures are nothing more than the teacher's or aide's activities. They are simply decisions regarding what it is that must be done to help students achieve the desired behavioral outcomes. Always remember that the instructional procedures are determined by the specific objectives. It is usually helpful to answer the following kinds of questions when determining the procedures to be used:

1. What is the student's role in the instructional plan?
2. What is my role in the plan?
3. What means of presentation will be used?
4. In what order will the activities take place?

Instructional Activities

The most important part of the instructional process consists of the learning activities. It is through involvement in these activities that student learning takes place and desired behavior outcomes are achieved. Activities must be interesting, challenging, and above all else, directly related to the objectives. Selected activities should represent a variety of learning approaches, including the auditory, visual, and tactile senses. Too often, reading is emphasized to the exclusion of other methods of learning, but listening to a story on a tape recorder can be an equally effective learning experience. Whenever possible, learning activities should take advantage of the variety of audiovisual materials now available in most classrooms.

Equipment and Materials

The decision on what type of equipment and materials should be utilized during instruction is dependent upon the decisions made in regard to the previous four components. However, learning materials need not be confined to either audiovisual equipment or textbooks. Field trips, local resource people, and research projects are only a few possibilities to consider when selecting teaching resources. You will probably also find that your teacher has a wide variety of materials available to you for the asking.

Evaluation

While the teacher aide is not expected to conduct a formal evaluation of student achievement, some type of feedback proves valuable in determining behavioral outcomes. Such procedures might include a brief question-and-answer period at the conclusion of an instructional sequence, or they might take the form of a short written quiz. Regardless of the method selected, evaluation helps you plan more intelligently for future instruction.

Format

The instructional plan on the following pages reflects the uses of the planning elements outlined above. You may choose to use this type of format, or you may choose to develop one that meets your particular needs. Regardless of your decision, you will find that the children in your classroom benefit from effective planning.

SAMPLE TEACHER AIDE INSTRUCTION PLAN

TOPIC: Review of Roman Numerals

OBJECTIVES: To review the Roman system of numeration. The student should be able to—

1. Compare the Roman system of numeration to our system with particular emphasis on rules for combining symbols.
2. Write standard numerals when Roman numerals are given.
3. Write Roman numerals for numbers less than fifty.

CONTENT: In the Roman system of numeration, the position of a basic symbol affects its meaning. If a numeral for a smaller number follows a large number, the number named is the sum of the numbers of the basic symbols. For example, the Roman numeral VII means 5 + 1 + 1, or 7. However, if a numeral for a smaller number comes before one for a larger number, the smaller number is subtracted from the larger one.

When a numeral for a smaller number comes before a numeral for a larger one, the first numeral must represent 1, 10, or 100 and so on. It must represent the largest such number that can be subtracted from the larger one. The only numeral that can come before V or X is I. The only numeral preceding L or C is X. The only one that comes before D or M is C, and so on.

PROCEDURE: Begin the lesson by asking the children to tell where they have seen Roman numerals. Some students may have seen them on buildings, in books, or on clocks. Discuss the uses of Roman numerals in today's world. Then review briefly the material contained in the content section of your instructional plan. Have students work each of the problems on a duplicated worksheet individually, then discuss the answers orally. After all of the students have completed the worksheet, place a list of Roman numerals on the chalkboard. Students will come to the board to write the standard numeral.

INSTRUCTIONAL ACTIVITIES

1. Students will work problems on the worksheet and orally discuss the answers.
2. Students will write standard numerals for Roman numerals placed on the chalkboard.

Students will make a list of ten standard numerals and exchange papers to have the second student write the Roman numeral for each.

EQUIPMENT AND MATERIALS

1. Duplicated worksheets with twenty-five problems
2. Chalkboard

EVALUATION: At the conclusion of the review lesson, each child will be required to (1) write the standard numeral when the Roman numeral is given for twenty numbers, and (2) write Roman numerals for numbers up to fifty.

ASSIGNED TASKS

The duties you are expected to perform as a teacher aide will probably encompass the entire gamut of school-related activities. However, no two aides experience identical duties. You will find that assignments vary according to the needs of the students and teachers with whom you work. However, the following list of typical duties may give you some idea of the tasks you may be asked to perform.

Instructional Tasks

1. Assist students in any subject area in which the teacher feels confident that you are competent
2. Read and tell stories
3. Collect and arrange displays for teaching
4. Assist students in performing activities that have been initiated by the teacher
5. Assist students who miss instruction due to absence
6. Assist students during library periods
7. Review, summarize, and/or evaluate learning activities
8. Listen to oral readings by students
9. Assist the teacher in special demonstrations
10. Conduct small group activities
11. Help slower students with their lessons
12. Assist with physical education activities
13. Correct homework and workbooks, using the teacher's key
14. Correct standardized and informal tests and prepare student profiles
15. Assist with supplemental work for advanced students
16. Assist students with written compositions, especially with spelling, punctuation, and grammar
17. Acquaint students with etiquette and good manners
18. Instruct in the safe and proper use of tools
19. Prepare instructional materials such as flash cards, charts, transparencies, etc.
20. Provide special help, such as drilling with flash cards, spelling, and play activities
21. Work with small groups or individuals under the teacher's direction in order to review work, drill, or do creative activities
22. Write exercises and number work on the chalkboard
23. Assist with and check students' seatwork

24. Help students find reference materials
25. Supervise student laboratory work

Clerical Tasks

1. Maintain attendance records
2. Maintain health record folders
3. Type reports and notices
4. Prepare stencils
5. Distribute materials to students
6. Prepare graphs and charts
7. Prepare transfer forms
8. Assist with daily reports that are sent to the office, such as those for milk, lunch, and attendance
9. Collect notes sent to parents when educational field trips are planned
10. Assist with registration of students on the first day of school
11. Collect, organize, and file materials for units of work
12. Collect and organize work turned in by students
13. Maintain individual folders on children's work
14. Type, duplicate, and/or collate instructional materials submitted by the teacher
15. Keep a record of class schedules
16. Keep records of books students have read
17. Average academic marks
18. Compile a list for teachers to use in the requisition of supplies
19. Enter evaluation marks in the teacher's record book
20. Keep inventory of classroom equipment, books, and instructional supplies
21. Manage classroom libraries
22. Type and duplicate the class newspaper
23. Duplicate students' writings and other work
24. Type and duplicate scripts for plays and skits

Audiovisual Tasks

1. Check out and return audiovisual materials

2. Prepare introductions to give students background for viewing audiovisual materials
3. Preview films and other audiovisual materials when requested to do so by the teacher
4. Set up and operate audiovisual equipment:
   a. Filmstrip projector
   b. Opaque projector
   c. Film projector
   d. Slide viewer
   e. Overhead projector
   f. Tape recorder
   g. Television
   h. Language master
   i. Microprojector
   j. Learning centers

General Tasks

1. Assist in preparing the room for instruction
2. Supervise students' cleanup time
3. Arrange instructional materials for accessibility
4. Mix paints for art activities
5. Prepare and supervise students' work areas
6. Supervise students in certain housekeeping duties
7. Check lighting and ventilation and make necessary adjustments when necessary
8. Monitor the administration of tests
9. Work with special programs such as dramatizations, puppet making, and assembly programs
10. Accompany groups of students when they attend special programs and take field trips
11. Supervise groups of students to and from their designated dismissal points
12. Assist the teacher during the lunch period
13. Help with decorations for special events
14. Assemble materials and equipment needed by the teacher and store them after each use
15. Help maintain bulletin board displays
16. Monitor the study hall

17. Accompany students to the office, clinic, etc.
18. Assist committees engaged in special projects involving construction, research, or experimentation
19. Supervise students' club meetings
20. Keep chalkboard clean and ready for use
21. Maintain orderly arrangement of the classroom
22. Administer routine first aid and attend sick and injured children
23. Supervise the loading and unloading of school buses
24. Distribute books and supplies
25. Help children with their outer clothing
26. Obtain materials for projects
27. Prepare and serve refreshments at snack time
28. Arrange interesting and inviting learning centers
29. Proofread the class newspaper
30. Monitor the classroom when the teacher has to leave it for brief periods
31. Help supervise students on the playground
32. Arrange and supervise indoor games on rainy days
33. Assist students in lavatory activities
34. Assist in supervising rest periods
35. Keep bulletin boards current
36. Assist with fire drills
37. Assist substitute teachers in planning work
38. Repair materials and textbooks
39. Assist in the supervision of children in the library
40. Talk quietly with a student who is upset
41. Help students settle arguments without fighting
42. Classify and organize instructional materials
43. Attend to the weighing and measuring of students
44. Display student work
45. Type and duplicate instructional materials
46. Keep a folder of representative work for each child
47. Supervise activities such as those found in programmed learning
48. Help students look up information in resource books
49. Help students move from one activity to another

HINTS FOR TEACHER AIDES

In order to help youngsters learn, the teacher and the teacher aide must work as partners to make their own relationship successful. The more skills you bring to the classroom, the more valuable you become as a team member. Usually, teachers are unaccustomed to supervising another adult. Therefore, your presence in the classroom can be an important asset, or it can cause the teacher more work than it is worth. If she finds it necessary to stop her work frequently to give you an assignment or to provide directions, then she is reducing the already limited amount of time she has to spend with students. Make sure your presence in the classroom permits the teacher to spend additional time with the children.

Of course, teaching is the most important task in which you can become involved. There are many ways in which the teacher can involve you in the children's learning. For instance, you can help one student while the teacher is explaining other material to the entire class, or you can help children at their desks while the classroom teacher instructs a small group of children. At times you can work with the entire class, freeing the teacher to confer with individual students.

Often a beginning aide experiences difficulty in learning to communicate and relate well with children. Some hints that may help you establish needed rapport with youngsters are given:

- Be yourself. Be warm and friendly. Children respond to a smile or a friendly pat on the back.
- Be firm and consistent. New aides sometimes overlook discipline in order to court feelings of love and acceptance from their children, but fairness and consistency are factors that earn respect.
- Show a sincere interest in the things children approach you with. Value them as they do.
- Be a good listener. Resist the urge to do all the talking. Children have all sorts of things to tell you.
- Be sympathetic and patient. Children have bad days too.

Perhaps they would like to talk to you about their problems.

Classroom management is another opportunity for you to become involved with the children. While some may think of it only as housekeeping chores, classroom management is much more than just keeping the room tidy. It is more concerned with the overall arrangement of the room — for example, making the bulletin boards, library corner, bookcases, and displays more attractive. However, classroom management can also mean such routine tasks as taking attendance, passing out art supplies, or collecting lunch money. The aide helps in these areas by freeing the teacher to concentrate on improving the quality of the learning experience, since she knows that her classroom management is in capable hands.

Playground, hall, and cafeteria duty are also excellent ways for an aide to become familiar with children's behavior. You see children in an entirely different light when you observe them outside the classroom. In a casual setting, the aide has an opportunity to observe children doing the things they want to do. What you learn in these situations can serve as a useful resource background as you work with your children within the classroom.

SUMMARY

Even though there are many functions for which the classroom teacher is legally responsible, these same functions can often be performed at some level by the teacher aide. While you are not expected to have either the skills or professional training of a classroom teacher, you can still extend and enhance the learning activities in which the teacher is engaged. Your contribution increases the teacher's sphere of action. You extend the teacher's hands, eyes, ears, and feet by the supplementary work you perform with the children. You add support to the teacher's efforts by taking over where she leaves off.

As a second adult in the classroom, you permit a greater focus on the individual learner than the teacher alone could hope to achieve. A teacher aide in the classroom gives the teacher valuable flexibility in organizing the learning program for greater individual educational experiences. If has often been said that the best learning situation in the world is one teacher with one student. More individualized instruction is possible if teacher aides are effectively utilized within the classroom.

CHAPTER 3

LEARNING ABOUT LEARNING

AS a teacher aide, it is extremely important that you have an understanding of how children learn and of how you may enhance their learning. As the study of learning is discussed, a number of questions should be kept in mind. What does learning actually mean? How can teachers and teacher aides encourage children's desire to learn? Are there specific underlying principles that make for a good teaching-learning situation? How does the satisfaction of certain needs affect the learning process?

"Children learn what they live." This truism indicates that teachers and schools are not the only influences upon youngsters and that learning is not limited to the classroom walls or even to teachers' objectives. Students learn from all their experiences, both curricular and cocurricular. In the classroom, too, learning is more than simply gathering and memorizing isolated facts; the child has many learning experiences, both direct and indirect, formal and informal.

It is through the learning process that children gain competence in using their resources for thinking, feeling, and doing. It is by means of learning that they eventually establish their unique selfhood. A skilled learner, in addition, is a resourceful, flexible person, one who is able to use what he has learned in new and unique situations. To develop such an individual requires an emphasis on the development of insight rather than of rote learning.

WHAT IS LEARNING?

Learning involves adaptation of behavior. Emphasis is on achieving behavioral change in the student, based on his personal and purposeful recognition of events, blended with his individual needs and goals. To be effective, learning must fill needs, meet personal objectives, and make the child more capable of coping with his environment. Goal setting by the learner motivates learning.

Most educators define the learning process as change in behavior resulting from the interaction of the child with his environment. Learning is dependent upon some activity or special training; in this sense, it differs from changes in behavior that are related to the child's level of maturity. Likewise, learning differs from changes due to maturity, in that modification of behavior patterns is a result of something external rather than of change within. Learning, then, involves more or less permanent behavioral changes, which are the result of a particular experience. Learning usually requires a change in perception, which in this sense is the manner in which the individual experiences his world.

A number of factors have a significant effect on the learning process. Particularly, you should be aware of the influences of parents, the maturation process, the social climate, and of individual motivation on the effectiveness of the learning process.

The Parents

Since a child's first teachers are his parents, they have a far greater influence upon his attitude toward learning than any other individuals with whom he has later contact. Most of his attitudes, values, and habits have already been established by the time he enters school. Certainly, parents provide the child with his first social interaction. Their attitudes toward learning are a model for him to accept or reject.

Parents, however, should not be expected to teach what professional educators cannot get across. While parents can provide a number of experiences and a great deal of support, they cannot be given the full responsibility for developing their child's interest in learning. For example, teachers should not assume that homework must always be checked by parents. Instead, the parents' responsibility is to have materials that promote learning available in the home.

Parental involvement in the learning process, both positive

and negative, should be considerable. The professional staff should investigate effective ways of establishing communication between the school and parents and should seek to assist parents in encouraging their children as they enter the learning process.

Maturation

The degree of maturity achieved by the child has a significant influence upon the efficiency of his learning. Numerous research studies have shown educators that learning is most effective during certain periods of the child's developmental cycle. Adequate development of maturity reduces the time required for learning. Likewise, learning is generally more efficient when the proper stage of maturity has been reached. Ideally, instruction and growth patterns should be in harmony with each other. Each child has a period of optimal readiness for learning. Instruction begun before or after that period usually reduces the effectiveness of his learning experience.

The Social Climate

It is important for an aide to realize that learning occurs in a social setting. She needs to learn that the classroom atmosphere is one of the most important factors in the learning situation. The type and amount of acceptance and approval received by the child, the emotional tone of the classroom, and the development of an attitude that encourages creativity are all vital to a good classroom learning environment.

It is also important, then, for both teachers and aides to recognize two influential facets of the social climate in learning. First, a child cannot be taught effectively unless something about the home environment, community, and social background, which help to shape his habits and values, is known. Second, teachers and aides must be aware of their role as the director of a group and the effect interaction has on the learning process.

Motivation

Another important factor in assisting children's learning is motivation. Motivation is the act of stimulating interest or of effectively using interest that is already present. The child can be exposed to knowledge; obviously, he does not always learn, regardless of the quality of instruction. In addition, he does not always learn exactly what the teacher desires.

All children come to school with varying interests. Determining the child's interests and working with them to increase learning are practices basic to successful teaching. It seems clear that when teaching a child, the child's own purposes and goals must be kept in mind. The more clearly the child perceives his goals, the more strongly his acts of learning are motivated.

RECOGNIZING INDIVIDUAL DIFFERENCES

Individual differences exist among children. Many differences, particularly physical ones, are obvious. However, in the areas of emotional and intellectual development, differences from one individual to another are just as pronounced as physical differences, even though they may not always be immediately visible.

Recognizing various individual differences is essential if you want to work successfully with children. You must strive constantly to identify the characteristics that your students possess and exhibit. Sometimes you will be limited to personal observation and subjective judgment as you attempt to understand your students, although, more likely, standardized test information is available to help you identify individual student differences.

In the process of identifying individual differences, the classroom teacher and aide have to consider several questions. Does the child learn rapidly and easily? Does he use common sense? Can he see relationships? Does he reason well? Is he highly observant? Does he express himself clearly? The teacher who can accurately assess factors like these is moving beyond the task of merely teaching a group of children and is beginning to meet individual differences.

Unfortunately, the range of individual differences is not likely to be significantly reduced by the learning experiences typically provided in some classrooms. No plan for ability grouping or any other technique or device can wipe out entirely the range of differences exhibited in any given group. Children at the various grade levels cannot be thought of as a single unit; the range of differences is a fact that must be considered, regardless of the degree of ability grouping that is present.

You will find that the extent of individual differences in a typical classroom is amazing. For example, in most elementary classrooms there are one or two students in the genius or near-genius classification and one or two students in the dull-normal or borderline-intelligence class. Between these two extremes is the remainder of the group. The differences are largely in the area of academic aptitude. However, you will find similar differences in motor coordination, social maturity, emotional stability, and physical condition.

Many teacher aides, and perhaps a few teachers, are unaware that these differences are perfectly normal and exist in every classroom. It is in this great variety of abilities and talents that we see the uniqueness of American education. Thus, the school makes a unprecedented contribution to the development of children, whether they become professional football players, scientists, business managers, or store clerks.

READINESS

A child learns best at that moment when he is ready to learn, not before and not after. Obviously, the key to effective and efficient learning is readiness. The idea of learning readiness implies that there is a particular time for all kinds of learning activities, a time when the student is emotionally and intellectually ready to learn at the maximum rate. Readiness also includes the interest and desire to learn, as well as the mental ability needed for the learning task. Educational psychologists say that readiness is determined by two interrelated factors, heredity and environment. Heredity sets the limits of the intellectual ability of the student, while environment determines how closely the child comes to having the opportunity of reaching his potential.

It should be recognized that developmental rates vary from child to child and that learning is most effective when the proper stage of maturation or readiness is reached. Readiness should not be thought of as occurring at certain periods, such as when entering first grade or moving ahead into junior high school, but rather it should be seen as a factor with which all who interact with children must be concerned.

The concept of readiness has several important implications for the teacher aide. First, since the environment is so important, the aide should attempt to provide the kind of positive experiences that build awareness and enable the student to best utilize his potential. More often than not, this process entails creative teaching and means individualized attention. Second, there is little value in trying to force a child to learn who is not yet ready either mentally or in terms of motivation. If the right time is waited for, the student usually learns rapidly and easily. However, this does not mean that if a student experiences difficulty with some learning task, he should be permitted to quit. Rather, it means that if the student and the aide have conscientiously tried several different approaches over a period of time, then a waiting period before another learning attempt is made might be warranted. Finally, teacher aides should be alert for the optimal period when the student is ready and eager to learn. The most effective teaching methods are those involving instructional materials and activities geared to the learner's readiness state.

An example of the importance of readiness is found in the area of beginning reading. Experimentation has shown that a child must have a mental age of about six years to begin to read successfully. Attempting to teach a child to read before he has reached this level of mental development is usually nonproductive. Under the stress of an adult's great desire for the child to learn to read, the immature child usually only parrots sounds or perhaps recognizes some sight words, but the concepts that the words symbolize have no real meaning for the child, and the rate of retention and comprehension is low. However, more than mental age is involved in reading readiness. A youngster must have developed mentally to a point where he can do some abstract thinking, can remember word forms, and can see likenesses and differences. Readiness to read is also related to the child's emotional, social, and physical development. Even so, he may not yet be ready to learn to read. Although he may be interested in the content of books, he may not learn to read as long as he can get some adult to read to him. There are many cases of bright children who failed to learn to read because they did not feel the need to learn. But, when parents or other adults stopped reading to them, the children learned to read on their own.

What is true of beginning reading is also true of other learning skills. There is little value in attempting to teach a child until he exhibits both the desire and the readiness to learn. However, it is also true that readiness to learn with no possible outlet is extremely frustrating to a child. The child who is ready to read should be helped to learn, just as the student who is ready for chemistry should not be asked to repeat general science courses he has already mastered.

MOTIVATION FOR LEARNING

In order for learning to occur, motivation is essential. Motivation releases energy for the task at hand and thus tends to direct behavior. There is no such thing as unmotivated learning. Sometimes the motive may be weak or poorly defined, yet it is always present. In the classroom, then, it is not just a question of whether or not the instructor motivates the child to learn; the only question is what methods are used to motivate the child's behavior.

You will find that the process of giving rewards and punishment plays a very important role in motivating children's learning. Positive reinforcement, or reward, whether it comes in the form of words of encouragement or whether it is something of material value, is a form of motivation. In most cases, the motives of the learner determine what is interpreted as a reward. If the child's goal is to gain support from his classmates, a good grade in spelling is interpreted as a reward only if good grades are also important to his peer group. Sometimes a youngster finds intrinsic reward by discovering meaning in something he has been striving to comprehend. A similar feeling results from the knowledge that he is doing well and is making progress.

Punishment or negative reinforcement, on the other hand, is based on fear, embarrassment, or loss of status. It may cause the child to become so fearful or embarrassed that either he does not respond at all, or he becomes hostile and unreachable. Punishment is a negative motive at best, and it never encourages creative activities. Nevertheless, many teachers undertake questionable actions that are intended as punishment; for example, arbitrary lowering of grades, sarcasm, or ridicule may be used as punishment. All of these actions should be seriously questioned as satisfactory motivational devices. Often, they produce the opposite effect than that which was desired.

In addition, two widely divergent approaches to motivation are available to teachers and aides. In connection to learning there is internal and external motivation. Usually motivation is referred to as *internal* if it lies within the act itself and *external* if the motivation is applied from without. The student who learns to play the drums because he wants to play the drums in the school band is following an internal motivation. He is following an external motivation if he learns to play the drums because if he does not practice, his father will punish him. External motivation is always based on the idea that individuals are seeking rewards or avoiding pain, whereas internal motivation is based on the premise that individuals are basically goal seekers.

Almost without exception, an individual who relies totally on external motivation believes that children will inevitably resist learning and therefore must be forced to do worthwhile tasks. The person who uses internal motivation proceeds on the assumption that youngsters naturally love to learn. Contact with children provides evidence that they do like to learn; in fact, children are full of questions that indicate their desire to learn. Children take both their desire and basic curiosity to learn to school with them and usually retain these qualities until unpleasant or unprofitable learning experiences cease to have meaning for them or fail to serve a useful purpose.

The following summary of motivational functions should be useful to the teacher aide:

1. Instructional materials should be personally meaningful and individualized to as great an extent as possible.
2. The attitude of the teacher aide toward the learner should include cooperation, trust, and recognition of individual differences.
3. To guide learning, you should always take into consideration the goals and purposes of each individual.
4. In motivating a child, it is important to consider his growth and maturation levels.
5. Some external motivations, such as rewards, may be used to encourage learning, but care should be taken that this method is not overdone.
6. Sincere praise and encouragement should be given often to each child.
7. An effort should be made to encourage a child's attitude toward his work to be based on his own internal motivations whenever possible.

INTERESTS

Motivation and learning are closely related to a child's interests, since as a youngster grows and develops, his interests widen and change. Effective motivation always takes into account the interest factors. It recognizes that interests can be created and that changes in behavior, as well as changes more directly related to learning, can be influenced by the creation and development of various interests.

Different kinds of home environments encourage widely different areas of interest to develop. For example, a child who grows up in the home of a college professor may develop a strong interest in books due to the fact that he was brought up in an environment that valued books. Similarly, a youngster from a family who has an active interest in sports usually has an interest in sports himself. Thus, to a large extent, children develop interests on the basis of their environment.

As a child develops and learns, his interests mature and broaden. In the early years, he is concerned only with home and family. Gradually, his interests broaden to take in playmates. Then, as a youngster's environmental influences are affected by different and far-ranging experiences, his expanding interests make it possible for him to have a richer education. New experiences bring forth new interests, and new interests in turn lead to new experiences. In addition, children's interests change as they grow older. A child of six may be interested in one type of television program or book, while an older child may be interested in a much different type of program or book. Therefore, interests are the products of both learning and maturity.

You will learn that some children can do a variety of things well, while others are successful in only a few. You should constantly probe the student's interests and abilities. For example, ask youngsters to respond to questionnaires that ask them to indicate activities that they enjoy most as well as those they do not enjoy; also seek to identify the activities in which they are successful and unsuccessful. Use the information gathered as you plan games and activities for large and small groups. Students who appear to have few interests and abilities should be placed in situations where they can explore new dimensions of their present interests and further enlarge their abilities.

As a teacher aide, you will learn that educational experiences that run counter to students' interests lead quickly to frustration and regret. Students who work against their own interests and abilities often turn out to be poorly adjusted adults. The wise teacher and aide study their classes' interests, capitalizing on these driving forces when working with the children. They help develop new interests by means of carefully planned field trips, as well as by other means of exposure to new environments. Parents also should be aware of their children's interests. They should realize that interests change and develop, not according to teacher or parental demand, but only as a result of additional learning, new environmental influences, and, of course, the normal maturation of the child as an individual.

EMOTIONAL CLIMATE

Among the basic needs of children, none seem to be more important than affection and security. From affection and security, children gain desirable recognition. The understanding teacher and aide know that the kind of emotional climate produced in the classroom affects the emotional adjustment of each youngster within the room. The sensitive teacher aide can do much to foster good mental health by helping to create a classroom environment that encourages children to adjust healthfully and cooperatively to the day-to-day life of the room.

Emotional development seems to be an individual matter. No two children ever react in exactly the same manner or make the same response to an environmental situation. Their temperaments, past experiences, personal reaction patterns, and individual personalities influence their responses. Whether a child responds with fear, anger, joy, or delight to a given emotional situation depends upon his past experiences, his present psychological condition, and his feeling of security. The child must be understood as an individual before his emotional growth can be guided.

Children can be assisted toward better emotional maturity when the channel of communication between them and the adults in their lives can be kept open. Youngsters must feel free to talk openly with their teachers or teacher aides. They must feel that when they have concerns, an adult who cares is also concerned and can provide them with opportunities for self-expression.

Teachers and aides also need to become more sensitive to the feelings of children. This requires knowing the way a child feels about his place within the group and also his feelings relating to his own personal successes and failures. Many students need a substantial amount of encouragement in order to feel confident and adequate within themselves. It is also necessary to find ways to work more effectively with children in order to encourage them to express their emotions in a positive way.

Likewise, the teacher and the classroom aide are probably the two most important factors in creating a desirable emotional climate for the child at school. In their hands is the opportunity to teach children to create for themselves the kind of personal world that has as little fear and tension as possible and as much security and tranquility as can be achieved. To create these desirable conditions, you must establish rapport with the children with whom you work. If children learn only to stay out of your way and to hide their problems, then there is little hope that the school will make a constructive contribution to their emotional well-being.

An understanding individual realizes that rapport is not a quality which, once established, can never be lost or improved upon. Instead, in your day-to-day working relationships, you will want to safeguard and preserve the positive rapport already established and to display characteristics that will make the children want to continue to value your further guidance as they develop, change, and mature.

Rejection is probably the chief menace to a child's feeling of security in the classroom. If a youngster is not fully accepted because of his racial or religious differences, his mental ability, his physical peculiarities, or his economic status, he senses that he does not belong. He is not secure; instead of feeling protected, he senses that he is openly vulnerable. The understanding aide must bear this in mind as she works with children inside as well as outside the classroom.

As you endeavor to provide security to the children with whom you work, you will find the following suggestions helpful:

1. Know not only the children's names but also much about their personal backgrounds, which affect their relationships in the classroom.
2. Be as consistent a personality in dealing with children as

is humanly possible.

3. Participate actively and naturally with children in what they enjoy doing — in their work and their play.
4. Demonstrate to the children that you believe in them and in their potentialities.
5. Create an atmosphere in which each child is free to be himself as well as free to let you see him be himself.
6. Give honest praise and reassurance for achievement.
7. Plan with children in such a democratic way that every child has the security of knowing that he has an important contribution to make to the class.

THE ROLE OF THE TEACHER

The classroom teacher who approaches the learning process from a developmental standpoint is primarily concerned with fulfilling the fundamental needs of the child in order to assist his maximal development within the classroom. To accomplish this, the teacher must understand the child's particular needs and unique growth pattern. When mass education loses sight of the individual and his development, it is not effective in producing academic growth. In education, the goal is not to turn out a uniform product but instead to accept the youngster as he is and to bring him to the maximum level that can be expected for him. A wise teacher is interested not only in how much the child learns but also in the kinds of attitudes that are being formed toward learning.

One of the most important and exciting challenges any teacher can face is that of thoroughly understanding each child in her classroom. As she comes to know him as an individual, an instructional plan can then be formulated. The well-trained teacher always has some basic understanding of each individual's purposes, assets, liabilities, and interests. Because the classroom teacher is also responsible for group learning experiences, she must understand the way in which each child fits into the group and then determine how the child seeks to belong to the group.

Likewise, it is basic to an effective learning atmosphere for the teacher to understand the general range of capacities within her classroom and to be aware of the wide range of learning experiences that are necessary for her children to achieve effectively. Since not all children learn in the same way, the teacher is required to adapt her teaching methods to meet the individual differences she finds in her class.

When the teacher truly individualizes her teaching approach, it gives her the opportunity to emphasize success rather than failure. This approach necessitates taking a continuous inventory of the child's growth status and altering her instructional techniques accordingly. One of the most urgent needs in education today is the provision of time for teachers to learn about each individual student and to assist in the development of appropriate educational plans. The teacher might assist achievement best by recognizing the importance of some of the following techniques: (1) attempting to meet the child's specific needs; (2) assisting the child in using new concepts and skills on a continuing basis; and (3) utilizing the ego involvement of the child in order to motivate him, using a minimum amount of threats and comparisons.

When the teacher understands that the children in the classroom ·comprise a unique set of growth patterns, her primary task is to understand the patterns and to attempt to harmonize instruction with the patterns, rather than to teach some mythical, average child. She realizes that at first she may not understand the pattern of all children, but through continual child study she can eventually develop competency in techniques that assist her in accounting for the major share of individual patterns that must be recognized and dealt with in the typical classroom.

Finally, the teacher must also recognize the variety of roles she must play in the course of her various contacts with children. The teacher is primarily involved as a director of the learning process. Each child and the significant factors affecting his readiness for learning must be understood. This process involves responsibilities in evaluating student progress and assisting students in developing self-evaluation techniques. Teachers also serve as specialists in content areas providing contact with the world of knowledge. Classes are groups; therefore, the teacher is a group leader who must understand group dynamics.

IMPROVING CONDITIONS FOR LEARNING

When the classroom instruction is well-planned with the children's interests and needs in mind, motivation for learning can be a comparatively easy task. School experiences should be consistent with the intellectual, physical, and emotional needs of the youngsters. Living and learning in the classroom should relate to the child's own world. He must feel that he belongs, and he must believe that he can achieve. Also, individual differences must be recognized, and meaningful experiences must be provided. Growth in desirable and worthwhile behavior characteristics must be the goal of achievement.

Many children fail to learn merely because they are discouraged. Discouragement usually stems from a child's lack of confidence in his ability to cope with problems. The child assumes that he cannot succeed; therefore, he anticipates failure. Some of his problems arise from early competition within the family. Other problems develop when excessive pressure is applied by significant adults in his life. To help such a child, his concepts and expectations of himself must be changed. Methods for helping him to overcome his fear of failure must be sought. Through encouragement, our faith in him as he is will be communicated. Additionally, encouragement enhances the child's self-respect. This approach gives recognition for effort, not just for achievement. Teachers and aides who use an approach of encouragement focus on the child's strengths and assets rather than on his weaknesses and limitations.

It is imperative that the child see meaning in the tasks he is asked to perform. In addition, he must have a clear understanding of what is expected of him. Ideas must be presented in as concrete a fashion as possible. The utilization of audiovisual materials is essential. Frequent review and thorough mastery of the material should be encouraged, as long as doing so does not approach the point of boredom. Competition among students should be discouraged; children should be encouraged to compete only with themselves and their past performance.

Likewise, a good classroom environment is free of undue pressure and strain. It should radiate excitement and involvement through the use of meaningful activities. An effective learning climate should lead the child to broaden his horizons, to be curious, and to ask questions in eager expectation.

The following qualities are usually in a good learning environment:

1. There is constructive interaction between the teacher (or aide) and the children.
2. The learning experience has importance for the youngsters.
3. The child is expected to do only that which is in keeping with his ability and maturity level.
4. Children are given opportunity for both individual and group experiences.
5. Each child is free to learn in his own way within the limits of the learning situation.
6. Opportunities are provided for children to recognize their own achievement.
7. Opportunities are provided for youngsters to evaluate their own achievement.
8. Children are given equal opportunities with adults to plan and carry out ideas and activities.

In your role as a teacher aide, you will work with many different children of various ages. Remember that students of all ages have certain characteristics in common, such as a need to be liked, to belong, and to achieve. However, at different age levels, unique behavior patterns appear that are closely related to the child's social, emotional, physical, and intellectual development. It is important for you to know general characteristics of children at a certain age and what kind of behavior you can expect from them in their normal course of development.

SUMMARY

In this chapter, some of the most important growth and development factors that characterize children's learning have been discussed. It is important to remember that these typical characteristics do not always fit the real child in an actual classroom. Every child follows his own pattern of development; however, these characteristics may be a guideline for determining aide behavior in the classroom.

The interaction between the teacher and students as well as the interaction among the students themselves is related to efficiency of learning. The students and teacher serve as stimuli for one another. Effective instructional methods as well as high and consistent achievement by the students is closely associated with warm, understanding, responsible, businesslike, stimulating, and imaginative teacher behavior. Regardless of other behavior, the teacher must be perceived by the students as a helpful person in order for progress to be made toward significant educational objectives.

CHAPTER 4

WORKING WITH CHILDREN

TODAY, the range of teacher aide activities in the classroom is as broad as the field of education itself. It is apparent that there is no school program — either curricular or extracurricular — in which aides cannot be used effectively. There has been not only an explosion in the number of teacher aides, but also a tremendous increase in the kinds of activities they do.

Years ago, teacher aides were limited to such nonteaching chores as overseeing the playground, taking attendance, and monitoring the cafeteria. Aides still perform these essential services, but today they also serve as indispensable assistants to the classroom teachers. It does not stop there. Today's aides find themselves directly involved in the educational process itself; they may tutor individuals, listen to groups of children read, or help children with their homework.

If the definition of the word *teaching* includes imparting knowledge, skills, and attitudes, then, as any teacher aide knows, it is hard not to "teach" by every action and word. Experienced educators agree that even those who are not formally trained to teach can still change a youngster's picture of himself and his attitude toward learning through effective tutoring. There is also evidence that aides can contribute to the general level of knowledge and to the increased development of learning skills of many students. The question of whether or not you will be able to accomplish these two worthwhile goals depends, at least in part, on the instructional skills you develop.

The experience of working directly with children in the classroom offers you many stimulating professional opportunities. You have a chance to broaden your educational perspectives as you test some of your pet theories by putting them into actual practice as you guide children in various aspects of their growth and development; and you learn more about how youngsters, as individuals and as groups, react and achieve in various school settings. In addition, your classroom experiences with the children provide many opportunities for stimulating your own growth, both as a person and as a paraprofessional. Practical experience enables you to learn, through observation and participation, more about the goals and purposes of schools. Working with the teacher in the classroom makes available to you rich experiences in the various aspects of the work of the teacher aide — experiences that would not be possible in any other way.

OBSERVING CHILDREN IN THE CLASSROOM

The way in which a child behaves and reacts in different situations tells the alert teacher aide many facts about him. For that reason alone, careful observation of children is an essential step in assisting the classroom teacher as she identifies those who need special help and guidance. It is not always easy to interpret a child's behavior accurately and precisely. Certain basic skills and a minimum amount of knowledge about child development are essential to this important task.

When observing youngsters in order to identify their needs, it is important to describe the different types of behaviors, abilities, or defects observed in such a way that no stigma or handicap is inadvertently placed on the child. Extreme care should be taken to see that names are not applied as permanent labels to the children so identified. For example, a label like *slow learner,* or *problem child* could do great emotional harm to a child if, in your eyes or his own, he is permanently tagged with this label. Using educational labels is helpful only if it stimulates and encourages help for children.

Our experience has shown that these difficulties need not present a problem and that this kind of unproductive labeling need not occur if two ideas are kept in mind. First of all, remember not to look at the child in terms of the labels but rather in terms of the behavioral characteristics that he shows. Secondly, remember that you are using the label only for your own purposes in order to help the child. In fact, any label is only a starting point used to assist the child; it is not a final edict that closes his case.

There are certain standard procedures that apply to all student observations. These four basic procedures are listed:

1. OBSERVE EACH CHILD IN A VARIETY OF SITUATIONS. In order to obtain as complete a picture as possible of each child's behavior, try to observe the child in different settings and at different times. As a teacher aide, you have an opportunity to observe youngsters in a variety of situations — in the classroom, during the lunch hour, on the playground, and at school social events. It is important to observe students in various phases of their school life, because it is common for a student to react one way in one situation but to react differently in another situation.

Observing children in a variety of situations also helps you to become aware of the special talents and abilities that individuals possess. For this reason, among others, children should be given a chance to display their abilities in such areas as creative writing, art, music, and dramatics.

2. GIVE EQUAL CONSIDERATION TO EACH CHILD ON EACH BEHAVIORAL CHARACTERISTIC. When you observe children for a specific behavioral characteristic, be careful not to overlook any child in the classroom. For instance, when you consider a characteristic such as, "Is not liked by other children," certain children may immediately come to mind, but on closer examination there may well be other children who exhibit this same characteristic. Most mistakes in observing children are made through careless oversight.

3. COMPARE EACH CHILD WITH THE REST OF THE GROUP. Comparing each child with the entire group as you seek individuals with particularly outstanding characteristics gives you, as a bonus, a good yardstick for also measuring his individual educational, social, and emotional needs.

4. BE AWARE OF YOUR OWN BIASES. Every human being is unconsciously biased against certain types of children. This human frailty is as natural as your liking or disliking for certain foods, clothes, or books. It is important to try to recognize

your own biases and to make allowances for them. For instance, you may find it difficult to say or even think something negative about a child whom you like. On the other hand, if you dislike a child, you may have difficulty seeing any good qualities at all in him. It is very easy to endow a likeable child with more positive qualities than he actually possesses while at the same time ignoring the same positive qualities in a less likeable child. The first step in helping any child is to make an honest, objective evaluation of his particular strengths and weaknesses.

Despite the fact that youngsters in a classroom often display distinct group characteristics that are unique to that particular classroom, it is unsafe to make sweeping generalizations about individuals merely from observing their group. While group behavior is often a common denominator of the conduct of many individuals, it does not accurately represent any given child. In order to plan and carry out a good instructional program, you must know each child as an individual.

You will be busy with a variety of tasks as you begin your work as a teacher aide. Getting acquainted with your assigned teacher and the other members of the staff, establishing a relationship with the children in your group, and becoming familar with the school routine could easily take all of your time and attention. Finding time to learn more about individual children is easier if you think in terms of the opportunities available during the regular school day. Some of the most appropriate times are suggested:

1. Observe the children in supervised activities outside the classroom, such as in the cafeteria, during assembly programs, or during physical education.
2. Observe children at their "free periods" when they are not closely supervised, such as before school, during recess, or after school.
3. Set up a systematic plan for observing individual students during regular classroom activities.

SHOWING A REAL INTEREST

The most important single characteristic a teacher aide needs is a sincere liking for children. That sounds obvious, yet it means more than just the usual automatic response. Truly liking someone means accepting him the way he is and maintaining a continued interest in him as a person. In most instances, the value of an aide's sensitive understanding of a child and the degree of empathy she communicates to the child far outweigh any lack of knowledge she may have in a particular instructional skill.

The sincerity of your interest and your respect for children cannot be faked. Your interest must be genuine. Children seem to have built-in antennae that detect the difference between a genuinely warm, friendly person and a person who merely puts on a show of friendliness without really feeling that way. For example, children are much better at reading body language than are adults. Youngsters are much more apt to watch what the aide does than to listen to what she says. "I have enjoyed reading with you," is a meaningless statement of empty words if you, at the same time, pull away from the child or won't let him put his untidy hands on the book.

When you talk with children, talk naturally and avoid a patronizing tone of voice. Adults who are not used to young children sometimes adopt a tone of voice that seems phony to the youngsters. Always think in terms of talking *with* the child rather than talking *to* him. Call him by his name. Write your name out for him on a sheet of paper to take home. Don't be surprised if, at times, he acts as if you are his mother or if he forgetfully calls you "mama"; in his mind, both of your functions are of a similar, supportive nature. Try never to disappoint a child. If, for instance, you have promised to take him to the library and you find yourself unavoidably detained, be sure to ask another aide to fulfill your promise. If you promise to bring him a book or magazine, don't forget it. He won't.

Many of the best ways of showing your interest in a child are relatively simple. One of the most effective methods is to simply listen to the child. Accept the youngster's ideas as worthwhile. If you are really interested in him, you will want to know what he thinks — what his favorite television programs are, what he likes to do with his father, or what his favorite sport team's mascot is. Ask for his opinion about a variety of things. Sharing his thoughts and feelings helps in two ways. Not only does he have an opportunity to talk with you as an equal, but the experience is bound to increase his self-confidence, since he cannot be wrong about his own opinions.

When the child is talking, don't criticize his language or interrupt him to correct his pronunciation or grammar. Instead, concentrate on the much more important fact that he is communicating with you. By the same token, don't put too much stress on formal manners. At times, most children are noisy or messy, put their feet on the furniture, or interrupt others. Accept each child the way he is; don't unnecessarily discourage him from being himself.

Expect some children to try to shock you with lies or street language. While you may be shocked, don't let it show. More than likely, it is their way of trying to get attention. So when such behavior shows up, set aside your lesson plan and pay attention to the child's needs for the moment. However, in the case of persistent discipline problems, ask your teacher or supervisor for assistance. In your daily interactions with children, don't try to become an amateur psychiatrist. If there seem to be serious psychological or emotional problems present, talk with your classroom teacher or counselor about them. Don't try to solve them yourself.

You will soon learn that children will test your professed interest in them. They may even try to "con" you. One teacher aide was prevailed upon by a child to give him lunch money. As a result, the child felt guilty about the incident and would have nothing further to do with that particular teacher aide. Likewise, it is usually best for teachers and aides to refrain from giving gifts or material rewards to children.

CREATING THE DESIRE TO LEARN

Many children who experience daily difficulty in the classroom suffer from dismal feelings of defeat. These feelings are enough to block any and all future learning. Many "slow learners" have become convinced of their inability to learn and have long ago given up even trying. They think of themselves as being "dumb" and of school as being a place that merely reinforces their relentless feelings of failure. They quickly withdraw from any situation that threatens to expose their alleged deficiencies. They soon find ways to avoid participating at all in the learning process. For example, if they have a choice of seats in the classroom, they may select one on the back row, or they may try to sit directly behind another student and thus try to become invisible. It is easy to sense when a child has decided to tune out and turn off. Then, according to the dictates of his particular personality, he may try to escape your notice, or he may resort to disruptive behavior.

The question must be asked, "Can teacher aides help to change this type of behavior pattern?" Yes! There is something special about the aide-student relationship. There is a more important difference between the teacher aide and the classroom teacher than just in the matter of teaching. Their aims are profoundly different. The classroom teacher's primary responsibility is to carry out the overall instructional program for a class of twenty-five to thirty children. The teacher must be concerned with such matters as curriculum choices and class schedules. The aide, whose sole concern is with the child who failed to keep up, is free to concentrate on something of equal importance in the educational process — the child's self-image.

As a teacher aide, your first objective is to help the child see himself as a person who *wants* to learn and as a person who *can* learn. Only after you achieve this first objective will you want to focus on subject matter and content. Your initial relationship with the child should emphasize establishing effective rapport. Often, when the anxieties and competition of the classroom are removed, youngsters learn that they can succeed, and over and over again they prove that they can do just that when given the right opportunity. Best of all, they suddenly find themselves with an adult who is interested in them as persons. The personal interest that you show in the children may be the ingredient that is needed to help them recognize their personal worth and ability so that they will feel motivated to achieve successfully.

It should have become apparent by now that one of your most important roles as an aide is to rekindle the child's natural desire to learn. This task, while far from being easy, is made simpler if you are alert to both the child's interests and his needs. For example, if the child is interested in airplanes, the two of you could check out a book on the subject from the school library. Give him a chance to explain airplanes to you. Quite likely he will not be able to read much of the book, but maybe he will let you read to him. You might want to borrow the book and rewrite some of the material in language he can read and understand. There are a variety of different remedial reading series available, written to combine a low reading and high interest level, that explore subjects of interest to boys and girls.

Learning experiences similar to the one just described can be readily constructed for students at any age level on any subject. They require only an understanding teacher aide who has the imagination and sensitivity necessary to find the proper clues that will help her find the spark needed to rekindle the child's desire to learn.

TUTORING

One of the best entry tasks for aides in the area of instruction is that of assisting individual students with drill exercises, especially for purposes of remediation. Most elementary and secondary school classrooms have students who need individualized remedial attention. Teacher aides can assume the task of supervising youngsters as they work independently in reading, spelling, math, and science. The responsibilities that aides can perform in these areas involve a variety of tasks, including helping students to improve special skills, listening to oral reading, and repeating teacher-prepared instructions.

In order to initiate the tutor's role in the classroom, the teacher must first identify those students who are in need of additional assistance. During classroom instruction, the teacher may observe a student who is having difficulty reading. Additional informal observations of that student's reading as well as the administration of an individual diagnostic reading test might indicate that the youngster appears to be having difficulty with vowel sounds and phonograms. The diagnosis might also indicate that the student's instructional reading level is approximately two years below grade placement. With this information, the teacher can direct the aide to use specific activities that have been especially designed to remedy the student's deficient skills. The teacher can also prescribe materials that are appropriate for the tutoring sessions.

A tutoring program should be designed to ensure that the youngster has the opportunity to succeed. He would not be in the program unless there was reason to believe he could profit from it. Yet the child may not believe he can be helped. You will have to convince him that he can succeed, that you believe in him, and that together the two of you will prove that he can be successful. It would be a good idea to use materials that do not seem like classroom assignments or remind the youngster of past failures. In fact, you may have to make some of the materials yourself.

The first step in the tutoring process is to find out where the student is in the subject in which he is being tutored. The teacher is usually the best source. She knows the child's performance level and has access to his test scores. She is also aware of the specific skills he lacks and probably knows the areas where he needs selected practice. You should always begin at a level well within the student's grasp and where he can succeed. When he is right, be sure to tell him so, but do not praise him for every little thing he does. Only honest and deserved praise means anything to children. Your attitude shows the child what you really think.

One stumbling block to learning for many children is the fear of making mistakes. Let the child know that everyone makes mistakes, that making mistakes is all right, and that it is one way to learn. However, do not let the child flounder. Step in and help him out before he becomes totally frustrated. When possible, it is best to let him find the answer himself. Discuss the lesson together rather than ask him to recall specific facts. Devote part of each session to activities that you know he does well and enjoys. A quick review shows him the progress he is making. Find ways to exhibit tangible evidence of his progress. As a youngster learns more words, for example, have him add them to an alphabetical list. Soon he will have his own little dictionary of words he has mastered. You could also put the words on index cards in a box and watch them grow day by day.

GUIDING GROUP WORK

Effective group work is not something that just happens. It has to be encouraged, developed, and nurtured by the teacher and the aide. Frequently, the teacher aide works with a small group of children rather than with the entire class. Such groups are assembled for any of a number of purposes. Small groups may be organized to provide specific help on a needed learning skill. For example, even though the children regularly read aloud in their reading groups, the teacher may note that three or four students are having difficulty reading aloud in an interesting, enjoyable manner. These youngsters might meet with the aide for several sessions to improve their oral reading skills.

Groups may also be organized to pursue a particular interest shared by several children. Most often, this relates to a topic or unit already being discussed, but it can also serve as a motivating device. For example, three boys with a specific interest in airplanes may prepare a report or display that contributes a great deal toward interesting others in this particular aspect of science.

To illustrate how an aide can assist with instruction, the case of a reading teacher who has been working with her class of third graders and who has already diagnosed the wide variances in the abilities of the youngsters is given. While the aide supervises the rest of the class as they work independently on suffixes, the teacher can select a small group of students for diagnosis. She may discover that the five slowest students in the classroom cannot function satisfactorily because they are still unable to recognize syllables in words. When she has diagnosed a common deficiency in the group, she can call the aide over to the group and give her specific instructions concerning remedial activities to perform with this group of children.

At this point, the aide's job is to reinforce and continue what the classroom teacher has already begun with the students. With the reading class, it may be a simple matter of giving children further practice in counting syllables and using words that have been divided into syllables. The aide can work closely with the students in a natural teaching situation, asking questions about correct pronunciation or answering questions about a particular step in the learning process.

Another example is a math teacher who has been working in some phase of general mathematics with fifth grade students. After identifying students who need help, she can then turn the group over to the aide for drill work. The aide, with specific instructions, can assist the youngsters in reviewing, for example, their multiplication tables.

One of the most valuable tools for group instruction is discussion. "Let's talk about it" instead of "Let me tell you" is the modern instructor's way of utilizing group experiences to improve verbalization. Discussion techniques encourage children to be inquiring, alert, and effectual thinkers when talking with others about problems and experiences. Today, many different kinds of discussions are in evidence in the classroom: teacher aide-led discussions, children-led discussions, panel discussions, forums, round-table discussions, and others.

In using discussion techniques with small groups of children, you will need to develop certain skills. The following suggestions may help you in guiding small group discussions:

1. *Ask questions at the appropriate time:* "What do you mean?" "Is that a fact or an opinion?" "How is that different from what John said?"
2. *See that various points of view are given an equal hearing:* "Who has a different idea?" "Bill, would you like to reply to what Betty just said?" "Is it all right for Gary to disagree with us?"

3. *Keep the discussion on the point:* "Let's get back to the subject under discussion." "That is a different matter, Bill."
4. *Help children to increase their vocabulary:* "What does *encourage* mean to you?" "Does anyone know another way of saying the same thing?"
5. *Work for the constructive expression of ideas:* "Could we restate that idea in a more helpful way?" "How might that be said so that we can understand the idea better?"
6. *Summarize periodically when definite progress has been made:* "Let's see what the main points are that we have covered so far." "Larry, will you tell us your understanding of this matter before we go on?"

Working with children in small groups that are organized for a variety of purposes and that exist for various periods of time is an important part of a teacher aide's job. However, work with small groups does not end when you have gained competency with them, because group instruction is an important part of each child's learning experiences.

INDIVIDUALIZED INSTRUCTION

The goal of individualized instruction is to provide each student with a variety of instructional materials and approaches to meet his own needs. Teachers need to provide individual students with opportunities to study and work apart from the entire group. Not only do youngsters need to develop some responsibility for their own learning, they also need to encounter challenges that bring forth intellectual inquiry and creativity. More often than not, group assignments that result in conventional homework deny students exciting opportunities for independent study and investigation.

The teacher aide can play an important role in all efforts to individualize instruction. Teachers find it almost impossible to work effectively with individual students if they have no assistance. An aide can be of assistance to the classroom teacher in two broadly defined areas. First, she can help the teacher to prepare the appropriate worksheets and learning packets, etc., necessary to keep youngsters working at their maximum pace. Second, if properly trained, the aide can actually work with groups of students or individuals under the direction and supervision of the teacher.

In addition, the properly trained teacher aide can effectively perform most of the routine tasks germane to individualized instruction. When she is properly utilized, the pitfalls of this type of instruction can be minimal. Records can be kept complete and up-to-date; children can be kept functioning at their optimum levels; a high degree of personal contact can be maintained with each student; the volume of necessary clerical work can be more adequately handled; and the teacher aide can apply her talents directly to those individuals who are more in need of her assistance.

For example, the aide can easily make a daily check upon the progress of each student, identifying and providing materials needed, clarifying questions or problems, administering evaluation techniques when needed, and maintaining the record-keeping system. Referrals of specific students can then be made to the teacher if reteaching is necessary or if academic assistance is required that is of such a nature that it demands the attention of a professional, trained individual. Thus, the aide can keep direct contact with each child so that individual progress is maintained and nurtured on a daily basis.

Although diagnosis and prescription are the responsibilities of the teacher, the follow-up and implementation of the academic program are within the grasp of most properly trained teacher aides. The aide can prove invaluable when assisting children in completing assignments and in doing drill work on, for example, basic mathematics or reading skills. If an aide has the skill to resolve a particular reading problem and the teacher can be occupied more profitably with another child, then this should be the plan. Individual instruction should never be the exclusive territory of either the teacher or the aide; rather, it should depend upon the individual skills of each one.

During individualized instruction, you might do the following:

1. Keep records

2. Pass out and collect student materials
3. Work with students as they use programmed materials
4. Assist students in understanding directions (oral or written)
5. Read aloud any material that students find too difficult
6. Assist in moving students from one activity to another
7. Play educational games with students
8. Visit the library to help students select books
9. Gather information about work habits of students
10. Use audiovisual equipment with students
11. Develop a bulletin board display with students

PROVIDING FOR INDEPENDENT STUDY

Closely allied with individualized instruction is the instructional procedure of independent study. Independent work activities are those which children carry out on their own with little or no supervision from the teacher or aide. Through such activities, you provide for children's specific needs and adapt instruction to the individual differences that are found in the classroom.

Self-directed learning activities that take place during well-planned independent work sessions have many values for the child. Each youngster can proceed at his own rate, apply what he has learned, enrich his own understanding, learn to use his time wisely, improve his work and study habits, and grow in the ability to work on his own. Likewise, opportunities are provided for the development of such qualities as self-reliance, initiative, self-control, and independent thinking. Many students discover new abilities and grow in self-confidence. In addition, some students may have the opportunity to pursue exciting individual activities or be stimulated to develop new interests.

Independent study activities enable the teacher or aide to deal with individual problems, as well as provide additional study and practice for small groups with common needs. During the time when some students are engaged in independent activities, the aide is freed to work with other children who need independent help. She can pinpoint difficulties and special problems, evaluate the growth of self-directed responsibilities, and give children needed relief from periods of directed concentration.

When initiating an independent study program in your classroom, the teacher or aide can —

1. Begin the activities with those students who are academically and behaviorally ready to work independently. Gradually, other youngsters can be brought into the program.
2. Team students who have complementary strengths and interests. The entire class can begin independent study at the same time using this buddy system.
3. Allocate a regular class period during the school day for students to work on their independent study projects.
4. Provide time for student conferences with you to discuss progress and problems.
5. Determine a time for students to share what they have learned from their independent study projects with the rest of the class.

The success of independent study programs is often determined not so much by the complete absence of problems but rather by how problems are solved when they do arise. These are some situations and problems common to all independent study programs. These should be recognized and provided for when planning such a program. For instance, some students may select a study topic with limits too narrow or too broad for effective study. If this should happen, it is probably wise to develop a set of questions that either limit or broaden the scope of the student's independent study according to his topic. Further, many students are too dependent on teacher or aide direction, thus defeating the purpose of independent study. If this should happen, explain the criteria for independent study to the child again. Set smaller or interim goals that the student can easily attain or provide continuous reinforcement for tasks completed independently.

Independent activities must not be considered simply busywork or time-consuming seatwork. Each activity should be planned with the same care that is given to other experiences within the school program. Specific plans should be made ahead of time for each kind of independent activity in the classroom.

For example, essential materials should be ready for distribution or be easily accessible to students. Directions for children should be checked for clarity so that each child knows exactly what is expected from him. Additional work suggestions should be planned for those who finish before the rest of the class. It is often fruitful to check the teacher's editions of basic textbooks in reading, mathematics, and other subject areas for specific suggestions regarding independent study.

Success in using independent activities is more likely in a classroom that is well organized. Clear and specific standards of classroom behavior are needed if disorder and aimless activity are to be avoided. Students should understand that it is both a privilege and a responsibility to work independently and that they should strive to accomplish their tasks without disturbing others, including the aide at work with other students.

The more carefully you and the teacher plan and prepare for independent study, the more effective you will make the total educational experience for every youngster. Always keep in mind the ability, the interests, and the needs of each child. Discuss with your supervising teacher her point of view on independent activities, and make your own plans accordingly.

WORKING WITH THE SLOW LEARNER

Most classroom teachers see slow-learning children as one of their most serious and demanding teaching problems. Because of their lack of grasp of subject matter, these students have a tendency either to ask many questions in an attempt to understand what is going on or withdraw completely from academic work without even trying to comprehend. The first child is a problem because of the amount of attention he requires; the second child is a problem because he refuses to even try to learn anything.

Just as the classroom teacher often looks at the slow learner as a problem, so the child looks at the teacher and the class-room situation as his problem. Perhaps you may not have looked at his point of view, but put yourself in the place of a child who is asked day after day to do work that is beyond his grasp and abilities. Try to understand and appreciate the problem of what it must feel like to make a determined effort to succeed at something, but yet to still fail. If you can empathize with the student in this situation, then you can begin to under-stand the reality of the frustration that is an everyday occur-rence in the life of a slow-learning child.

If you hope to help a slow-learning child, then you must examine certain basic attitudes that affect both you and the child. First, do you accept the child as he is? This precept is fundamental in regard to all you do for him. You must accept the fact that his learning problems are not his own fault. You must also realize that many behavior problems of slow learners arise from their inability to meet the demands made upon them. Few teachers or aides would criticize a physically crippled child because he cannot play football with the other children. Yet, many people criticize a slow learner because he cannot keep up with the more mentally able children within the classroom.

Second, how well does the child accept you and the school environment? You may have to be prepared to deal with the slow learner's negative feelings toward the school and toward teachers in general. More often than not, many of these children find the majority of school experiences unpleasant. If the child is in the fourth grade or above, his negative attitude toward teachers and school may be quite fixed, and it may be difficult to help him develop positive feelings. The younger child may not have had as many years to become bitter and unhappy about school experiences. Regardless of the grade level, however, your goal is to help the child accept you and the school.

Finally, do the child's peers and classmates accept him? One of the best ways to help the youngster gain acceptance from others is to help him develop his strengths and correct any faults that he can. The slow-learning child may excel in certain sports; he can be helpful and cooperative. Try to build on these abilities. This helps him to be accepted by his peers, and in turn his peers help him to accept himself. Much more emphasis must be placed on what the child can do than on what he cannot do.

Finding materials suitable for the slow learner's interest and social maturity level may be one of your biggest challenges. The difficulty of the material has to be in keeping with the child's mental age, while the content must be in keeping with his level of social maturity. Remember that the slow-learning child can be taught most successfully by means of experiences that involve physical activity rather than through reading and the use of abstract symbols. It is much more difficult for slow learners than for normal-ability children to utilize written materials and to grasp abstract concepts and ideas. For this reason, plan to make your instruction as concrete as possible.

The following list of identifying characteristics may help you to identify slow learners in your own classroom. The slow learner —

1. Is unable to think abstractly or to handle material that uses symbols.
2. Lacks the so-called common sense and reasoning level of other children his age.
3. Is unable to work independently.
4. Has a short interest and attention span.
5. Consistently withdraws from the group.
6. Breaks rules of conduct and is often unaware of it.
7. Is easily confused.
8. Has a poor attendance or tardiness record.
9. Is significantly below grade level in school achievement.

USING GAMES IN THE CLASSROOM

Educational games make learning fun for almost everyone, including children. An enjoyable way to transmit knowledge is to make a game of the subject matter under study. As a result of the fun and pleasure that games give to children, the game activities reinforce learning. Most children are anxious to learn drill activities if the activities are in the form of a game. Such experiences are pleasurable to the students when they get a chance to interact with their peers.

Games can also be used to satisfy children's emotional needs. A game and its related play activity provide a safe release for feelings of aggression or tension that may build up in children during regular school activities. Games interspersed with other classwork at frequent intervals during the school day aid youngsters who are extremely tense and need an opportunity to relax. Educational games that provide needed emotional outlets for children are important methods of maintaining good classroom discipline.

Game activities encompass a wide variety of forms. They can occur informally between two students, or they may be organized as activities involving opposing teams. Games can, on occasion, involve the entire class or they can be used with only a small group. Whatever the organization for the game may be, there are some basic procedures an aide should follow.

When utilizing educational games in the classroom, the teacher or aide should first decide on the teaching objectives and the scope of the subject matter she wishes to have included in the game activities. She must identify the learning problem and then select a game that helps the children understand the concepts to be taught in the game. Too often, instructors select a game to be used and then hope that the youngsters will learn something from it. An educational game should be used as an effective teaching device, not merely as something to fill in a class period. For instance, your teacher may discover during a reading lesson that the children are having trouble in discriminating between the different vowel sounds. She may then select a game activity such as *Vowel Bingo* and have you play the game with selected members of the class.

Second, before students begin to play the game, they need to know the rules and regulations that are to be followed while playing the game. Youngsters often become frustrated and unhappy because the game rules have not been fully explained. It is usually helpful for the teacher or aide to play the game first; then she can better explain the game to the children. With primary-aged children, the game rules and scoring procedures should be kept simple. Older children can usually be involved in complicated games with more elaborate rules. It is important to remember that game rules should be kept as simple as possible, regardless of the age of the children.

Third, all the children need to be actively involved in the game's activities. You will find that most educational games are designed for maximum participation by the children. A helpful way to include as many children as possible might be to start a pair of students in the game activities, then divide the remaining students into additional parts and add them to the game as it proceeds. Dividing the groups and adding new children to the game can be continued until all children are participating in the activity. Student involvement is an essential ingredient for game activities where youngsters can learn by doing.

Finally, most educational games are designed in such a way that a child can win or, at least, reach some goal or reward. However, for some children, the reward is learning subject matter in a nonthreatening activity. Even if the game organization includes having a winner or loser, the loser has the reward of reinforced learning.

The mental curiosities, capacities, and interests of present-day students demand that the teacher and aide go beyond the traditional textbook approach in order for optimum learning conditions to be present in the classroom. Thus, games and specialized learning kits are becoming an increasingly more important part of every school curriculum.

SUMMARY

One of the best entry tasks for teacher aides in working with children is that of assisting individual students with drill exercises, especially for remediation. Often, students need individualized, remedial attention. Competent aides can be given the responsibility of supervising youngsters who are working individually in reading, spelling, science, mathematics, or wherever an instructional activity requires adult supervision. The tasks that teacher aides can perform in these situations involve a variety of chores involving everything from accompanying students to the library to assisting with the selection of individualized materials in the learning centers.

As an aide, your primary function and responsibility is to increase the teacher's effectiveness within the classroom. You can expect the teacher to ask you to assist her in the preparation, presentation, and culmination of classroom activities. In your position as a teacher aide, you should be permitted to be more than simply a clerk or bookkeeper. Your usefulness should be limited only by your capabilities and by the ingenuity and management skills of your supervising teacher.

CHAPTER 5

DISCIPLINE, MANAGEMENT, AND CONTROL

Almost invariably, the successful teacher has a love for people — a love for people en masse, as well as a love for people as individuals. A teacher aide's feelings must be of a similar nature, for there is no substitute for the quality of caring. If you do not enjoy being with youngsters, if they make you feel uncomfortable much of the time, or if you are afraid of them, then being a teacher aide will never be much more than just a job to you — and an unpleasant job at that.

Achieving good classroom discipline and creating a proper learning climate are possible only if your self-image and role expectations are based on a positive mental attitude. If a poor self-image makes you feel inadequate to perform the tasks you are asked to assume, whether the task is teaching math or sewing a dress, you will have to work extra hard to overcome your feelings of inadequacy and try to build a more positive self-image. In order to instill confidence in others, you have to appear confident in yourself. "How," you may ask, "is this possible?" One rather simple but practical solution that works well is to plan effectively. Plan your lessons carefully and completely. Never leave anything to chance.

Planning for effective discipline involves planning ways to help youngsters move from external control by an adult to inner self-direction. However, most teacher aides are more interested in getting on with the task of tutoring or teaching students so that, more often than not, they consider time spent discussing routine matters such as rules for movement within the classroom or procedures for going to the bathroom as a waste of time. Sometimes, it may take an entire class period to properly establish a workable routine for asking questions or for coming to the teacher's desk for help. Since these interruptions can be both annoying and time consuming, it is important to impress upon students that the particular class routine or rule that you are seeking to implement is necessary if the class is to run smoothly. Once the routines have been well established, the time spent on planning will be saved many times over during the remainder of the school year.

CLASSROOM MANAGEMENT

In every classroom, there are certain details that must be taken care of regularly. Distribution and collection of materials, taking children to or from the classroom (individually or in groups), cleaning chalkboards, and keeping work space neat are only a few of the usual daily routines. In order to make the best use of your time, such regular duties should be managed in the most efficient and economical way possible. To accomplish this goal, the children and the supervising adult should work together to identify essential routines and then plan time-efficient ways of handling them. After your plans for handling the classroom routines are operating smoothly, the worries of carrying out these duties should be dismissed from your conscious attention so that your mind will be freer to adjust quickly to ever-changing classroom conditions.

Occasionally, other kinds of routine duties occur that do not demand your attention every day; such events may include receiving guests in the classroom, conducting fire drills, taking care of physical injury, and attending assembly programs. Even routines that occur infrequently should be discussed with the children, and plans for dealing with them should be made. It is always important that youngsters know what the proper procedures are in such circumstances and how to carry them out.

An important responsibility of the teacher aide is to become familiar with the classroom procedures used by the supervising teacher. There are many established classroom routines that you will want to adopt and use as you work with your group. This does not mean that you will want to mimic or copy every thing the classroom teacher does. Rather, you should determine which procedures you feel comfortable with and seek out the approval of your classroom teacher when you want to modify her procedures to fit your own personality. By quickly mastering a few basic routines, you will have more free time to use for beneficial planning, developing, and evaluating learning experiences for children. Likewise, you will avoid the minor disciplinary problems that sometimes arise when teachers fail to take care of routine procedures.

Let us consider some aspects of classroom management that seem especially important for a beginning aide. Some of these techniques are suitable only for older children, but most of them can be used at all levels of the elementary school. The following list should help you increase your efficiency in classroom management.

1. Assign specific seats to students in order to reduce the time required to take the roll.
2. Have students collect the distributed materials and papers.
3. Place books, materials, and equipment where students can reach them.
4. Post rules and regulations where students can see them easily and often.
5. Make certain that all students can hear what is being said in class.
6. Call on individuals by name rather than waiting for volunteers to answer a question.
7. Correct some work in class. By doing this you cut down on your own "homework" load; in addition, you can get students' papers back to them more quickly. Spelling papers and workbook pages, especially, are well suited for in-class corrections.
8. Use the "in basket" and "out basket" for handling assignments.

In addition, classroom management should be looked upon as definitely contributing, either positively or negatively, to the education of children. With this consideration in mind, students, teachers, and aides must work cooperatively in carrying out their necessary tasks. Promoting active student participation and encouraging healthy student attitudes facilitate the

CHECKLIST OF CLASSROOM ROUTINES

Directions: Mark each item of routine on the checklist as follows: If the item is entirely satisfactory, place a check (√) in the last column opposite it. If the item needs attention, place a cross (+) in the first column opposite it.

Routine	Needs Attention	Satisfactory
Calling the class to order		
Taking the roll		
Making announcements		
Collecting money for lunch, etc.		
Regulating room temperature and lighting		
Obtaining books, supplies, or other materials		
Caring for appearance of shelves, bookcases, etc.		
Beginning all activities promptly		
Distributing all materials and supplies promptly		
Collecting all materials and supplies promptly		
Removing waste from desks and floor		
Caring for chalkboard appearance		
Caring for bulletin board appearance		
Caring for overall general appearance of the room		

accomplishment of each person's goals.

The successful management of a classroom provides students a great variety of experiences that give them the opportunity to develop valuable social skills such as cooperating with other students, accepting responsibility, and strengthening other positive character traits that have carry-over values into other areas of school life.

Remember that the rules and procedures established by your supervising teacher have been found to work well with the children in your room; in many instances, the children themselves will have assisted in setting them up. Therefore, resist the temptation to make unannounced changes in routine. An unexplained deviation from standard operating procedures usually creates confusion. Knowing established routines thoroughly gives you added confidence and helps to convey a favorable impression about you to the youngsters. You might find it useful to utilize the checklist on page 81 to guide your handling of routine procedures in the classroom.

INTERACTION OF PERSONALITIES

The social climate of a classroom is determined largely by the degree of harmony achieved as individual personalities interact with one another within the group. The growth and progress of any youngster in the class in some measure affects the behavior of other children within the same group. Although the total effect produced by the various characteristics that make up an individual determines his so-called personality, certain specific aspects of personality can be profitably examined.

One of the most important personality traits of a teacher or aide is her evident and sincere concern for each child. Many people feel a genuine concern for others but fail to show it. All teachers and aides should notice little things about students so they can make positive comments about them when given the opportunity. Perhaps Patrick has combed his hair neatly or Jeff has brought an insect for the class to see or Carol has on a new sweater. The positive effects of a friendly greeting, a helping hand, a pat on the shoulder, or a word of encouragement cannot be measured, but such actions are valuable, concrete ways that show one sincerely likes and is concerned for individual students.

Having a pleasant voice quality, dressing appropriately, maintaining satisfactory personal grooming habits, keeping physically fit, and avoiding irritating mannerisms are some other desirable personal characteristics that teacher aides should cultivate and maintain. For instance, an aide's voice is usually most pleasant to listen to over a long period of time if it is relatively low in pitch and just loud enough to be heard comfortably by everyone in the classroom. The beginning aide will do well to practice speaking slowly and with a show of confidence, even if she does not feel that way inwardly.

You will find that children respond well to an aide who occasionally comes to class with a new dress or hairdo. In one class a quiet youngster came unobtrusively to an aide's side, stroked the sleeve of her new dress, and said softly but earnestly, "I like your new dress." Less shy children may quite normally be expected to ask the place of purchase or even the price. An aide who cares about her clothing and personal habits is usually more effective in promoting similar habits and attitudes among the students with whom she works. Remember that children expect aides to look and act like mature, professional adults: their actions and appearance should not cause them to be confused with high school students.

Quite often an aide's personal mannerisms of speech or actions are so amusing and easy to mimic that students entirely overlook her many good qualities. If you have doubts about the way you come across to students, ask your supervising teacher or another aide to point out your potentially offensive or distracting mannerisms that need to be avoided. Beware of irritating habits such as overusing certain words or phrases ("okay," "you know," etc.), pacing back and forth while talking, or chewing on a pencil or your fingernails. A calm, soft-spoken, self-assured, sincere, pleasant person is the most likely person to be successful in instilling these same characteristics in children.

Since it gives most children a feeling of security when they sense that an adult has confidence in them, more often than not they respond favorably when you show by your words or actions that you have confidence in them. One second grade teacher told the youngsters in her classroom that they were old enough to walk unsupervised to the school cafeteria. After they did so, they were proud to report how well they had done. Naturally, you must use good common sense when you make a judgment regarding who is ready to try something on his own. Children typically respond to the trust of an aide, especially when confidence is shown in them in a variety of ways.

When a well-meaning teacher aide finds student control difficult, often it is a result of her own inconsistency. Children like and respect firm, even strict, aides, provided they are consistent and fair from day to day and from student to student. Youngsters need the security of knowing what reactions they can expect from their teachers or aides when various activities are undertaken. Consistency can usually be achieved by establishing and maintaining clear classroom standards and by planning carefully in order to stay within your guidelines.

Finally, accept the children as they are. Recognize that there are likely to be wide variances in your students' abilities to make wise judgments and to control their emotions. Therefore, you may occasionally find it necessary to deal with some youngsters in ways that are less than ideal. For instance, a child may need to be forcibly restrained from hurting himself or another child or from seriously impeding the work of the group. Not only do children need to grow in their capacities for self-discipline, but you also need to improve your own ability to meet various kinds of unexpected classroom situations.

DEVELOPING RAPPORT

Rapport is the close, harmonious, sympathetic relationship that develops between individuals or groups of individuals. Every aide should seek to develop just such a relationship with each student. Good rapport is fairly simple to achieve when you are working with only one classroom of twenty-five or thirty children, but it is considerably more difficult to achieve when you are dealing with one hundred or more children who are located in different classrooms. However, when dealing with troubled or troublesome children in any class, there is no substitute for good rapport, which, when firmly established, can be a highly effective method of helping children to improve their behavior and to achieve better self-control.

How can you develop this rapport or closeness? Try sitting down and talking with the child or, more importantly, listening to the child — not while the rest of the class is doing seatwork, but at a time when other children are not around. Perhaps the two of you could have lunch together in the school cafeteria or possibly you could meet informally during an unassigned period. The child will be well aware of the fact that you are giving up your free time in order to talk with him. A word of caution, however — never arrange your time together immediately following misbehavior of the child, or he may inadvertently form the impression that bad behavior is rewarded by extra attention from you. Rather, arrange your "rap" sessions in between disciplinary situations. Begin in a positive manner by saying something like, "We seem to be having our ups and downs. Why is it we can't get along? What can we do to improve the situation here?" Sometimes the youngster will open up and tell you what is troubling him. Often he may not, but don't give up; keep trying. Give him plenty of time to think over his answers to you, and don't ask too many questions. Show him you are not angry with him but that you are puzzled and concerned by his behavior. By asking questions casually, by showing the child you are interested in him, and by convincing him you want to help, you can eventually win over even the most hostile child.

Psychologists tell us that love bolsters a child's self-confidence. Ideally, it should come from his parents, but in the classroom teachers and aides must often act as parent substitutes. Do not be afraid to show your love for children. Such simple gestures as sharing a smile, using a gentle tone of voice, showing sympathetic feelings when a child is in distress, or putting your arm around a child are wordless evidence to him that he has worth and importance in your sight. The spirit of love that your actions impart will become contagious, and you will be building such a class rapport that it, in itself, will be a magnificent lesson in human relations.

Does this mean, then, that you will permit a child to "get away with murder"? Certainly not! When he misbehaves, call him to your desk and whisper something to the effect, "You are letting me down." This technique is particularly helpful if the student has previously made a magnanimous showing of promising to cooperate in the future. Usually the youngster will apologize for his misbehavior and begin once more his attempt at better self-control. Unfortunately, some days nothing seems to work, and a troublesome child will try your patience to the utmost degree. Just remember that often the most unlovable child needs your love the most.

These are but a few of the many ways an ingenious teacher aide can achieve rapport with her children. If you are interested in better rapport with your present students, you may want to evaluate your answers to the following questions:

1. How often do you greet the children with a smile?
2. Do you treat every child the same way? Are there some children whom you allow to assist you more often than other children?
3. How often do children stop just to talk to you?
4. How do you encourage children to discuss their problems with you?
5. How often do you engage in small talk with children or discuss their day-to-day interests and activities with them?
6. In what ways have you attempted to draw out the quiet, shy children who are easily overlooked in the classroom?

PROMOTING EFFECTIVE DISCIPLINE

If you are like most teacher aides, you have an active interest in the word *discipline* and what it implies. Actually, the word has a variety of different meanings. However, as you are concerned with discipline in your work, it will usually be used to mean *orderly conduct*. In fact, you may use the terms interchangeably. But there are many ways to look at orderly conduct within the classroom. Does it mean student behavior that is controlled in an authoritarian manner by a series of rules and regulations laid down by the teacher or aide? Does it mean group controls cooperatively and democratically developed with the children for the purpose of creating a classroom environment in which each child can work effectively? Or, does it mean a happy combination of the above two methods?

When teachers, aides, and children work together in setting their own purposes, an environment is created that invites and encourages well-disciplined students. Try it and see how well it works. When you are dissatisfied with the conduct of individual children or of the entire group, examine the situation carefully to discover the possible causes for your dissatisfaction. In most cases, you will find that remedies for misbehavior do not lie in simply punishing the child or in becoming more authoritarian. Usually, the remedies are found when a more cooperative attitude on the part of the youngsters is developed.

Two kinds of behavior problems you may meet in your work as a teacher aide call for special attention. The first is related to the fact that you are an aide rather than a regular teacher. Children of all ages, knowing that you are not a teacher, will test you. They will come up with incredibly devious means to discover your ability and your expectations. When this happens, accept their actions as normal behavior and work toward the goal of establishing a positive relationship with the students. The most successful way to develop such a relationship is not to set out to make the children like you. Rather, improve the aide-student relationship by showing the children that you respect them, that you have a sincere concern for their welfare, and that you are prepared to provide needed help.

The second type of special problem that confronts the teacher aide relates to administering corporal punishment. Although school districts differ from place to place regarding school board policies concerning administering corporal punishment, most districts do not give teacher aides permission to paddle students. Even if your school district does not place restrictions on aides' use of corporal punishment, it would be wise for you to refer children who need such punishment to the regular teaching staff.

Your experiences as a teacher aide will be far more happy if you are able to view discipline in the ways suggested. From the beginning of your work in the classroom, try to take a positive approach in the area of discipline, and work dilgently on those activities that encourage children to regulate their own behavior.

Regardless of the ages of the children, the location of the school, or the specific duties assigned to you, children are more likely to cooperate with you if you keep the following guidelines in mind:

1. Help the student or students evaluate the problem situa-

DO'S AND DON'TS OF EFFECTIVE DISCIPLINE

DO

DO get to know the students by name early in the school year.

DO be honest with students.

DO encourage the cooperation of parents.

DO stop small problems before they mushroom into larger problems.

DO use group peer pressure to change undesirable behavior.

DO take time to consider problems as they arise.

DO be dignified and firm; expect cooperation from students.

DO anticipate behavior problems and correct them before they become serious.

DO forget the matter when a discipline problem is settled.

DON'T

DON'T force a child to apologize to you.

DON'T try to talk with a child until he has "cooled off" enough to talk rationally with you.

DON'T punish the entire class for the misbehavior of a few students.

DON'T use sarcasm or ridicule as a means of punishment.

DON'T make unreasonable demands of students.

DON'T use students to vent your own feelings of hostility.

DON'T hold grudges against students.

DON'T threaten students.

---

tion. Give them the benefit of the doubt.

2. Be calm and objective.
3. Keep your sense of humor.
4. Determine the facts rather than listen to opinions.
5. Take the offender aside and speak to him in private.
6. Separate your attitude toward the student from your attitude toward the behavior. Make him see that it is his behavior that is being criticized, not his worth as a person.
7. Do not make a big deal out of a trivial issue.
8. Help children to set their own standards of conduct in various situations.

The manner in which you handle misbehavior has a great

deal to do with how much satisfaction and success you achieve in the classroom. Children need to be treated firmly but with dignity by the teacher or aide who is in authority. Youngsters need the security of knowing that a responsible person is in control and that there are limits to acceptable behavior. In addition, when students do misbehave, the issue will be settled with much less antagonism if the students feel they have been treated fairly and if they have been helped to understand that certain consequences naturally follow certain actions. Certainly, little learning can occur, and few solutions to problems can be found at a time when students are upset or brimming with hostility.

Approaches to discipline that may appear at first to be effective are such tactics as demanding an apology, using threats or sarcasm, or punishing the entire class in retaliation for the deeds of a few. Actually, however, the negative effects of such approaches far outweigh any value that may be ascribed to their use. Youngsters react differently to the above techniques, depending on their cultural backgrounds, their ages, and their individual personalities. While the use of sarcasm may be successful in deterring a timid or sensitive child from a given action, more often than not, it will also result in permanent damage to your relationship with him. The teacher aide who uses sarcasm when dealing with a young child is taking unfair advantage of someone who lacks the skill to defend himself with a similar weapon.

Threats, similarly, are usually inappropriate and self-defeating, serving only to create unproductive feelings of apprehension and anxiety in the child. A threat hangs like the sword of Damocles over the errant youngster's head. However, the same sword also hangs over the head of the aide who makes the threat, and often she ends up being more severely punished than the intended victim. A threat, of course, is meaningless unless it is followed every time with the promised punishment. An aide who threatens detention for students who talk out loud may find herself stuck regularly as a prisoner in her own classroom during recess periods. The wise teacher aide avoids the use of threats.

WORK TOWARD SELF-DISCIPLINE

No matter which procedure you employ in dealing with discipline, work toward the goal of developing self-discipline in your students. However, don't expect them to reach this goal during the same year in which you work with them. Self-discipline is assumed to be present in adults, but it is only hoped for in children. Above all else, a self-disciplined person is aware of and responsive to the needs and rights of others. He is capable of establishing goals and working effectively toward them. He practices self-restraint without external direction when the need arises. He displays common courtesy as a matter of course. It usually takes at least the entire twelve years of formal schooling to develop these and other traits of maturity in individuals.

One basic misconception that some teachers suffer from is that they can develop self-discipline in their students by leaving the class alone for periods of time under the control of another student whom they appoint. However, this does not develop self-discipline. It merely substitutes a poor imitation of a teacher or aide for the real thing. You can develop self-discipline in students by leaving them alone from time to time, but do it by really leaving them alone. Don't turn on the intercom in the office while you are gone or appoint one student to take wayward classmates' names. Initiate your exercise in classroom self-discipline by briefly stepping out of the room while the children are occupied with seatwork. If your class continues to work satisfactorily at the assigned task while you are gone, you can then expand the length of time you are out of the room. When you leave your classroom, announce that you will be in the classroom next door or in the office, and then leave. Later on, leave the room while your students are occupied with a variety of tasks in which not all are working at their seats. Finally, permit small groups of students to work on projects outside the classroom without supervision.

One of the best opportunities for students to develop self-discipline is on the playground. Usually, children will establish and organize their own playground games and activities with a minimum of direction from adults. Look for evidence that your students are growing in self-discipline, and, conversely, note the behavior patterns exhibited by children who lack self-discipline. For example, which children always push to be first? Which ones are overly concerned about whose turn it is or about the length of the other children's turns? Which ones make excessive demands regarding the use of playground equipment? If you have a large number of students who seem unwilling to cooperate or share, develop the activities that encourage them to work together for the good of the entire group.

You will find that a child who is succeeding in his schoolwork is rarely disruptive. Therefore, try to build a success pattern with each child you work with in the classroom. A few basic rules might prove helpful in this regard. First, encourage the children to ask questions and to show you any work of which they are particularly proud. Walk around the room, glancing at each youngster's work. Troubled children often respond well to this type of attention. Second, avoid making negative or disparaging comments to children. It is much better to say to a child, "I know you can do better," than to say, "This work is poor." The former statement is gently encouraging, while the latter is painfully disheartening. Finally, be sure that your instruction is of value to every child. The intellectual food you prepare should be both palatable and digestible.

CONSTRUCTIVE PUNISHMENT

Most of the discussion to this point has focused on creating a classroom environment that minimizes discipline problems. These suggestions should help you to assist students in further developing their self-discipline. Inevitably, some youngsters lack inner control, and some classroom or playground incidents require disciplinary actions involving punishment. When dealing with such situations, it is extremely important for you to be aware of some of the requirements necessary for achieving and maintaining good discipline. It is also important to know how to use disciplinary techniques constructively.

Constructive punishment or discipline teaches children how to handle similar situations that may occur in the future, but at the same time it avoids the negative feelings associated with traditional forms of punishment. Your primary goal is to forestall a recurrence of the misbehavior that would make additional punishment necessary. In order for punishment to be a constructive learning experience, the student must understand and accept the punishment. Further, it must have meaning for him and make sense to him. In order for this to happen, the punishment should be imposed as soon as possible after the misbehavior has occurred, and the punishment should relate directly to the misbehavior.

The punishment should fit the crime, so to speak, and, when possible, the punishment should be a natural consequence of the undesirable behavior. For example, if a child throws a paper on the classroom floor, he should be asked to pick it up immediately and deposit it in the wastebasket. First of all, your responsibility is to assist the child in understanding why he is being punished; second, you should help him to plan his future actions so that he will avoid recurrences of the same undesirable behavior.

In addition, if the child is to understand and accept your punishment, it must be suited to his maturity level, to his unique personality, and to his individual needs. A first grade student who is told to refinish his desk after cutting it with scissors has neither the skill nor interest span necessary to complete the task. However, he could be assigned to help someone older accomplish the same task.

The student's attitude toward you is another factor that influences whether or not he will accept his punishment and learn to change his behavior. There must be mutual respect and trust between you and the child. If misbehavior takes place in the classroom, the rapport you have been able to develop between yourself and the student influences how he reacts to punishment. Showing a personal concern for the child and demonstrating a sense of fairness are essential elements in constructive punishment.

Many experienced teachers and aides have found the following specific suggestions for achieving constructive punishment useful:

1. *Discipline must be based on "do" rather than don't."* Emphasis within the classroom should be on practicing correct habits and responses.
2. *Discipline must be directed toward changing student behavior.* Since it is impossible to have a classroom where nothing ever goes wrong, we should be concerned about the manner in which students are dealt with when problems do arise. Effective disciplinary techniques successfully neutralize situations where disruptive misbehavior exists; student attitudes that promote learning in an orderly classroom environment are encouraged.
3. *Discipline must be based on cooperation.* Modern discipline methods require a considerable amount of cooperation between teachers and students.
4. *Discipline must involve a high degree of student participation.* If students have a major role in creating the conditions under which they work, they are far less likely to cause disturbances.

As a teacher aide, you should cooperate with the classroom teacher to help establish constructive discipline. Remember that, in the final analysis, what works for one individual may not always work for another. Each aide has to work out her own methods of maintaining effective discipline. Thus, the ideas in this chapter should be considered only as suggestions, not as ultimate procedures to follow in every situation.

ROUTINE DISCIPLINE PROBLEMS

Anyone who has worked with youngsters for a long period of time is aware that certain kinds of behavior are repeatedly displayed in the classroom by students. Even in a classroom with a well-prepared teacher aide, there are inevitably instances of unacceptable behavior. The guidelines presented here should help you to handle such situations with a minimum of conflict and will at the same time enable you to retain the trust and respect of both teachers and students. These guidelines should provide you with a practical "first aid kit" to help you cope with some of the most common disciplinary situations.

PROBLEM: Rowdyism upon entering the classroom

SUGGESTIONS: Place yourself near the door inside the classroom in order to direct student traffic. Speak in a pleasant and cheerful manner to students entering the room. In a moderate tone of voice, caution students who are pushing or causing a disturbance. Be quick to notice new clothes, neatly combed hair, or other remarkable details deserving your attention or recognition; avoid negative comments. Always have an assignment for students to begin upon arrival in your classroom.

PROBLEM: Undue disturbance during work or play periods

SUGGESTIONS: Begin to correct the situation by getting the students' attention. Discuss standards of behavior for the activity involved. Change assignments or rearrange group membership if necessary. If difficulty continues, withdraw a troublesome youngster from the group and have him work or play by himself. Later, when you have better group control, let him resume the activity.

PROBLEM: Tattling

SUGGESTIONS: Remember that the child who tattles probably needs friends and is attempting to win you as an ally. However, the act of tattling soon becomes part of a vicious circle. The more the student tells tales, the less likely he is to be accepted by the other children. Refusing to listen to the tattletales and making an effort to help the child become better accepted by his peer group are two positive approaches for improving this frustrating situation.

PROBLEM: Bullying

SUGGESTIONS: The bully may also need attention. It is likely that in order to satisfy his need to belong, he is using aggressive behavior to gain respect and admiration among his peers. Obviously, the bullying must be stopped for the well-being of others. If your verbal appeals to him fail, then correcting such behavior may require physically separating the bully from his intended victims. You may want to change his seat in the classroom or even specify an area on the playground where he is to remain during play periods. If difficulties persist, it may be necessary to seek the help of the school counselor or the principal.

PROBLEM: Defiance

SUGGESTIONS: Generally, it is unwise to overlook defiance. In addition, it is usually wrong to try to deal with it in front of an entire group of children. The wise teacher or aide asks the defiant child to step into the hallway, where she lets the offender know that he must follow her instructions or be prepared to take the consequences of his actions. Then she should be sure to follow through. If defiance is anticipated, it might be helpful to discuss the situation with your supervising teacher before you are left alone with the group.

PROBLEM: Rudeness and profanity

SUGGESTIONS: Do not show horror at hearing the street language that may be the customary vernacular for many children in your classroom. If only one child is involved, it is probably best to have a private conference with him; be specific as to what behavior you consider unacceptable. Follow up this conference with an in-depth study of the child to try to determine the likely reasons for his rudeness or profanity. Perhaps he is only compensating for a feeling of social insecurity, and, if so, you may want to help him find more acceptable ways of gaining status. If the majority of the group demonstrates rudeness and profanity, you may find it helpful to include the entire group in a general discussion about courtesy and how the practice of it is more profitable to the group than is the continued use of rude language and profanity.

PROBLEM: Cheating

SUGGESTIONS: As a general rule, cheating occurs when the pressure put on children to succeed is higher than they can tolerate. Therefore, not only the failing student, but also the high achiever may be guilty of this act. As a teacher aide, you probably will not be in a position to structure learning situations so that cheating will be unnecessary, since the responsibility for teaching lies within the teacher's domain. However, when it comes to daily work, you may well be in a position to encourage students to ask for assistance rather than to cheat. Perhaps you can arrange to have students work in groups where they exchange information while working on a group project. On tests, however, cheating cannot be tolerated. Usually the teacher has established rules regarding punishment for cheating, and you will, of course, follow these rules.

PROBLEM: Rushing or pushing when dismissed from class

SUGGESTIONS: Near the end of the class period, notify the students that it is time to start putting away materials and cleaning up their desks. Reward the students who have assumed an orderly position by dismissing them first; you may want to dismiss a row or table at a time as you see that all the members are ready. You will want to stand near the door. If the hallway from the room to the playground is a source of continuing trouble, escort the students outside.

SUGGESTIONS FOR TEACHER AIDES

Specific suggestions regarding classroom discipline, which have been made by a group of teacher aides, themselves, conclude this chapter. The aides who have provided these suggestions have had considerable experience in working with children on all grade levels.

1. Learn class standards, the daily schedule, regulations for the use of materials, and classroom routine early in the school year, and adhere to them when working with students.
2. Observe and follow the disciplinary measures used by your supervising teacher; make adjustments only after a conference with your teacher.
3. Try to handle your own disciplinary problems, but if serious problems occur, seek advice and help from your supervising teacher.
4. Set a good example for your students by always showing respect for your supervising teacher, principal, and other school personnel.
5. Use praise frequently and openly; find fault privately.
6. Be fair consistently; never punish the entire group for something done by only one or two students in the group.
7. Be helpful and courteous to all students; show a sincere interest in their problems.
8. Arrange individual conferences with troublesome stu-

dents so that constructive suggestions for improvement of their behavior can be made in a clear and helpful manner.

9. Use the school day for work. It is far easier to maintain discipline when students are busy at tasks they feel are worthwhile than when large amounts of class time are devoted to "busywork."
10. Provide a variety of activities, alternating vigorous physical activities with quiet activities or rest.
11. Refrain from embarrassing students by making pointed suggestions in front of others. Strictly avoid using sarcasm or ridicule.
12. Avoid being over friendly. Excessive behavior in this regard may cause students to misunderstand your actions and come to the conclusion that you are a "softy" or a "pushover" or that you feel unsure of yourself.
13. Avoid exhibiting a belligerent I-dare-you-to-do-it attitude that may challenge some students to try you out to see if you are "for real."
14. Select children who get along well together when organizing committees or work groups.
15. Keep your own mental health on a high level by getting plenty of rest, keeping your sense of humor, being attractive in appearance, and asking for assistance from others when you need it.

SUMMARY

Maintaining good discipline and helping students develop their own techniques for improving self-discipline are important responsibilities for all who are involved in the education of children. As a teacher aide, you are a member of this team of educators. In order for the school to operate effectively, the adults who direct its educational program must create and maintain a high level of quality, which will, in turn, lead to increased respect and prestige for your school.

There are certain basic techniques or methods for working with children who cause problems. First, you must be aware of

the cause-and-effect relationships involved. Children's misbehavior can usually be attributed to specific reasons; if you can
determine these reasons, you can often eliminate poor behavior
and also help the child to develop better self-control over his
behavior. The most important action that an aide can take to
help a troubled child is to establish a warm, close relationship
with him; the term *rapport* describes this relationship. After
you have developed rapport, you are in a position to determine
the root causes of a child's misbehavior, and you have a far
better chance of dealing effectively with him.

CHAPTER 6

READING AND THE TEACHER AIDE

EFFECTIVE reading skills are essential for success in school. Look over a list of the subjects that most schools offer, and you will find that reading is an activity in every class from the first grade through college, including all subjects from agriculture to zoology. Likewise, a great variety of reading is necessary for adults too — on the job, in business, and in the home. Reading is truly an indispensable skill. Job success often depends on how quickly and accurately meaning can be gotten from the printed page by the reader. The ever-increasing amount of printed material available today makes rapid reading with full comprehension a virtual necessity.

In addition, reading has an infinite variety of personal and social values for both children and adults. Good citizenship is largely dependent on gaining knowledge and understanding of this complex world. Knowledge, in turn, is dependent upon reading; and of course, effective reading depends upon understanding, remembering, and evaluating what is read. Reading also promotes personality growth by broadening interests. Certainly, it is an important part of life from childhood through old age.

Not to be underestimated are the rich satisfactions that come as a result of leisure-time reading. Such reading for pleasure and entertainment can be a major key that opens doors to the past as well as to the future. Vicariously, children as well as adults share through fact and fiction the interesting and exciting experiences of others, the young and old, rich and poor, famous and nameless. Through reading, books satisfy almost every taste and every mood.

In most classrooms today, teacher reading is considered a developmental process. It begins with prereading readiness activities and gradually culminates in fully developed, refined reading skills on the secondary level. In its primary stages, learning to read involves learning sight vocabulary words, developing structural analysis and word-attack skills, and improving comprehension skills for more meaningful reading.

OVERVIEW OF READING

Reading in its simplest terms is the act of comprehending meaning that is expressed in written language. Man first learned to speak and later to represent his spoken language by means of a code. Written language, then, is a code for spoken language. Reading is the reverse process; that is, the translating or decoding of graphic symbols into an oral language. Therefore, decoding requires that the reader perceives the separate sounds of the spoken language, then perceives the symbols that represent the sounds, and finally relates one to the other.

Before you can teach reading successfully, you have to realize that there is no one "best" approach to the teaching of reading. Rather, you should be aware of the advantages and disadvantages of each of the various approaches and then use what you consider to be the best of each approach. Each child is unique; therefore, he will learn to read by utilizing the approach or approaches most meaningful for him. Both classroom teachers and aides should be familiar with a variety of approaches to the teaching of reading. The major methods by which children are taught to read include the following:

BASAL READING APPROACH. The basal reading approach is the most widely used approach to the teaching of reading. This method is built around a coordinated set of materials that provide both a systematic and sequential approach to the development of reading proficiency. Such a program is constructed so that through the use of the basal reader, workbook, and other coordinated materials, the youngsters are given numerous opportunities to learn word recognition skills in a variety of ways. The primary objective of a basal reading approach focuses on guiding development through scope, sequence, and organization.

The major advantage of the basal reading approach is that it provides such a variety of excellent materials that it is easy for the teacher or aide to follow the reading manual in series, daily, month after month, thereby using the basal approach as a foundation on which to build other reading experiences As with any other reading approach, its effectiveness is dependent in large measure on the proficiency of the instructor.

LANGUAGE EXPERIENCE APPROACH. The language experience approach to the teaching of reading uses the child's oral language as the basis for his reading instruction. It recognizes that learning to read is largely dependent on the child's oral language background. In a language experience approach, the youngster's own language is recorded by the teacher or aide. Obviously, this approach uses words and sentence structures that are familiar to the child since they are patterned after his own speech. This familiarity with the written language motivates and aids him in reading.

The language experience approach to reading is built on the premise that the child's experience in the various language arts areas before he enters school and during his school years is the determining factor in how well he will progress in his reading. The teaching method used by the language experience approach is usually stated as:

> What I can think about, I can talk about.
> What I can say, I can write.
> What I can write, I can read.

INITIAL TEACHING ALPHABET. The initial teaching alphabet (ITA) is not really a method of reading instruction but rather a tool to be used by the teacher, regardless of the reading approach she chooses to use. It is simply what the name implies, an alphabet. ITA is designed to simplify beginning reading by eliminating the discrepancies between the forty or so sounds in the English language and the more than 2,000 varied spellings that represent these sounds. A one-to-one relationship between the letters seen and the speech sounds heard is the result. There is only one letter character for each sound.

After she, herself, overcomes the difficulty of learning the unfamiliar initial teaching alphabet, the teacher's main role is implementing the alphabet into the total reading program.

This alphabet is used only for beginning readers. The teacher must decide when each child is reading well enough in ITA to transfer him to traditional reading material.

INTENSIVE PHONICS APPROACH. The phonics approach to reading teaches word recognition as a sound-blending process. It emphasizes the use of phonics as the most important word-recognition technique. Through the use of this approach to instruction, the youngster is taught beginning sounds of words, vowel sounds, consonant sounds, and phonic blends. Teachers who use an intensive phonics approach may use one of several popular phonics workbook series, or they may use a basal reader with supplementary phonic instruction.

Using the methodology employed in the phonics approach, the children are taught the sounds of letters and how to combine or synthesize the sounds into words. The process always begins with individual letters and progresses to words. It continues with words that the children know; from these words, generalizations are drawn on the basis of similar phonic elements, and then new words are introduced using these elements.

INDIVIDUALIZED READING APPROACH. In the individualized approach, most of the reading materials used for instruction are published materials of various types. The teacher's role in this technique is that of a diagnostician and prescriber. The teacher must have basic goals outlined and specific skills identified prior to beginning such a program. Skills may be taught to the entire class, to a small group, or to a single child.

In the individualized reading approach, each child selects his own reading materials, sets his own pace, and keeps accurate records of his progress. Using this approach to reading, each youngster reads widely from materials of his own choice. Once or twice a week, the teacher meets with individuals for five to ten minutes. During the conference time, the teacher or aide determines what the child has read since the last conference, evaluates by means of carefully chosen questions the degree of comprehension, and makes note of special needs or difficulties. Then the teacher or aide, together with the child, decide his future choice of reading materials.

READINESS FOR READING

Admittedly, there has been a neglect both in the home and in kindergartens in providing sufficient intellectual stimulation for young children. Educators are aware that many homes fail to offer children the variety of needed stimulating experiences that nourish reading readiness and provide the basis for later success in school.

Teacher aides can help children prepare for reading in a variety of ways. They can help provide the kinds of experiences that have proved valuable in reading-readiness programs designed for young children. The following suggestions are relevant for both teachers and aides:

1. *Give a young child a wealth of varied experiences.* He will be reading about many different topics in school, so give him firsthand contact with real objects and varied experiences that will stimulate his senses. Let him observe and learn on trips and excursions to a museum, the zoo, a farm, and so on. Talk about what you see. Exchange ideas. Answer his questions.

2. *Be patient with questions from youngsters.* Faced with an almost endless barrage of "why," "what," and "how" questions, you may feel that even the patience of Job isn't enough, but your answers to his questions are important. He is looking for information that will explain and help him understand the world around him.

3. *Help the young child learn to listen to stories and to enjoy them.* Read him stories that he can understand and enjoy. Provide picture books and stories suitable for his age and maturity level. Let him handle books by opening them, closing them, and turning the pages. This helps him develop a real feeling for books and increases his ability to enjoy them.

4. *Remember that children naturally want to learn to read.* Give each youngster a chance and he will notice how wonderful and fascinating books and other printed materials are. Youngsters are as eager to learn to read as they once were eager to learn to talk and eat by themselves. They want to grow up, and reading represents a step in that direction.

Only gradually do some children come to fully understand that reading is a rewarding investment of their time. This is especially true, now that almost every child has ready access to the medium of television, which so easily preempts his time and attention. It would be much easier to teach some children to read if only more of them believed, deep down, that learning how to read was a genuinely worthwhile endeavor. Children are not persuaded that reading is a rewarding experience by merely being told that it is. The only persuasion is by such actions as reading to them regularly over the years, listening to them read aloud, and letting them see adults reading newspapers, magazines, and books for pleasure.

The literature of a culture is one of its most precious possessions and one of its most important resources. Children are not taught universal truths by talking about them, but adults can help children learn and assimilate these truths by reading to them or by guiding their choice of books. Through literature, children gain a greater awareness of other people who live lives much like their own as well as of others whose lives are very different from their own. Through reading, they can come to know their contemporaries better, as well as those far removed in time and place. Moreover, they can come to gradually understand the human condition with its astonishing variety and common concerns. Finally, though certainly not least in importance, the time spent reading to children can be a special, pleasant, relaxing, and rewarding time in the classroom. Unfortunately, in many schools today there is little time set aside during the day just to read for pleasure.

It should be remembered that the basic requirements of a reading readiness program include varied and extensive experiences; abundant opportunities for suitable language expression; a friendly classroom atmosphere; and the presence of an enthusiastic, capable teacher and aide. Under these conditions the child soon becomes ready to discover the wonderful world of books.

DIAGNOSIS OF READING DIFFICULTIES

Obviously, highly sophisticated skills or a scholarly understanding of the reading process are not required to determine that a child has a reading problem. Even a lay person can easily detect the unfortunate youngster who cannot recognize simple words or who seems unable to understand what he reads. However, in order to effectively assist a child who is learning to read, it is necessary to acquire much more detailed and specific information to help you or the teacher determine the best methods and materials to be utilized with the child. Almost always, the success of an instructional program closely reflects the quantity and quality of the time and care taken when making an initial analysis of the child's learning problem.

When an aide takes on the assignment of working with a child with a reading problem, it is important for her to have access to as much information as has been possible to accumulate. Since each reading problem represents a child's past failures, it is important to gain a basic understanding of what experiences the child has had that have led to his various areas of success and failure. Most frequently, school records are the primary source of such information.

Many schools administer individual diagnostic reading tests to all students. However, these tests must be administered to one child at a time, and some degree of skill and experience is required of the examiner. Such tests give information about specific deficiency areas. In addition, they allow the examiner to observe the child's reading habits and to make judgments about certain aspects of the child's reading ability that are not easily discerned under group testing conditions.

One of the most useful diagnostic tests of this nature is the *Durnell Analysis of Reading Difficulty* (Harcourt Brace Jovanovich, Inc.: New York), which measures both oral and silent reading; in addition, it includes the areas of phonetics, listening comprehension, word-analysis skills, letter recognition, and spelling. Graded reading passages make it possible to estimate oral and silent reading levels as well as performance in a variety of other aspects of reading. Three different reading levels are determined for each student. These levels, in order of reading difficulty, are referred to as follows:

1. *Independent level:* The individual is capable of handling

the reading material on his own without help from the
teacher or aide. The independent level is the level at which
the child should be reading when he is reading for pleasure and enjoyment.

2. *Instructional level:* A youngster, under supervision, reads
   to extend his skills in word analysis and comprehension.
   Ordinarily, it is at this level that the teacher or aide works
   with the child.
3. *Frustration level:* The reading material is too difficult for
   the student. It is highly unlikely that feelings of success
   will result from reading material at the "frustration" level;
   therefore, frustration-level reading is to be avoided whenever possible.

Another important source of diagnostic information is a
simple test of isolated sight words. Such a list may be teacher-
made, derived from a basal reading series with a representation
of the reading vocabulary found from the preprimer level to the
seventh or eighth grade level. More often than not, basal readers
list all new words introduced at that particular level in the
accompanying teacher's edition. A random sample of twenty or
twenty-five words for each reading level may be created by
simply dividing the number of words required for a good list
into the total of number of new words available at a particular
level. Using this method, if there were 200 new words in
all, every tenth word would be selected for the sight word
list.

Finally, both oral and silent reading skills can be determined
by an informal reading inventory. Taking a reading inventory
usually consists of having the child read short preselected passages at various level of difficulty that have been taken from
books of known readability levels. The passages should be of
sufficient length and content to obtain a satisfactory sample of
word recognition and comprehension skills at each level
checked. The inventory should contain two passages at each
level — one for oral reading and one for silent reading.

Many tests and inventories are available to assist teachers and
aides in determining the needs of students in relationship to

specific reading skills, as well as for determining the level at which effective reading instruction can begin. Both standardized and informal procedures are desirable, but the strengths and weaknesses of each must be thoroughly understood. Testing should never become an end in itself, but rather it should be a means of creating an effective individualized instructional program.

BASIC TUTORING PROCEDURES

Once you or the classroom teacher has diagnosed a child's reading problem, then you can begin either initial or remedial reading instruction. There are many effective techniques for teaching children the basic skills in reading, but underlying each of them is the common need for well-planned, sequentially developed instruction.

Plan intensively for your reading sessions with students. Although you may find it necessary to rearrange some of your planned activities in order to take advantage of fortuitous, spur-of-the-moment teaching situations, which present themselves unexpectedly, you will get more mileage from the time you spend with students if you have prepared worthwhile activities and materials. Likewise, try to meet as often as possible with the students. Five days a week is highly desirable but often is impossible. Two days a week should be minimal; meeting once a week is better than nothing, but is limiting because there is almost no opportunity for reinforcing new learning. As would be expected, most reading specialists emphasize that your chances of success with a child increase with the number of times you work with him each week.

Limit your reading sessions to no longer than forty-five or fifty minutes. It is wise to end the session while the youngster is still interested and wanting more; stop before he loses interest and is bored to death. You will find that you can accomplish much in forty-five well-planned minutes. Remember that many of the students you are working with in reading have a history of failure. They will have better success with you if you do not overtire them. The reading material you select, the activities you provide, and the length of your tutoring sessions should be geared to creating and maintaining a positive attitude in the student toward reading, thereby increasing his chances for success.

Several different kinds of reading activities should be included in each instructional session. The number and kind of activities you provide should depend on the child's attitude, attention span, and specific reading needs. No one prescription to be followed in every case can be written for you. Let your own intuition be your guide in determining how many activities you need to have prepared and how long each activity will last. One specific suggestion can be made — stop an activity whenever a youngster becomes bored and restless. Also, experienced aides have found that it is a good idea to have more activities planned and ready to use than you think you will need.

Many teacher aides report that they find a variety of good suggestions for reading activities in the teacher's edition and workbooks that accompany basal readers. Even though you may have to adapt some of the ideas to fit the needs of your own students, you will find that many activities can be used verbatim. The teacher's editions may also be useful in helping you to develop a sequence for teaching skills and to determine methods of reinforcing new reading skills.

If you are working with a student on developing word-recognition skills, you should know some basic principles of teaching word recognition. Here are some suggestions you may find useful.

1. Since each basic technique of teaching word recognition has certain inadequacies, teach the child a variety of ways of recognizing words. No one word-recognition technique applies to all words in the English language. The skilled reader must learn to shift, almost automatically, from one word-recognition technique to another. For instance, he might use phonics to sound out *cat*. However, if the individual tries to use phonics to decode a word containing *ough*, he would soon run into diffi-

culty, since he would have no way of knowing whether the *ough* had the same sound as the *ough* in such words as though, thought, through, tough, or bough. Therefore, to decode the word containing *ough,* he would have to shift to other techniques; he could use context clues plus the sound of the initial and/or final consonants to infer the word.

2. Always introduce new words and new techniques gradually and with enough repetition so that the learner has a growing sense of mastery. Most basal readers provide about ten repetitions of a newly introduced word and five repetitions of previously introduced words per story. It has been estimated that the average child requires from thirty-five to forty repetitions of a word in order to recognize it quickly and accurately.

3. If the child needs additional drill on recognizing certain words, try to provide it in a variety of ways in order to avoid boredom. One technique that has worked well for us is to have the youngster make up sentences using the word. Write down the sentences and have the child read them out aloud. Then divide the sentences into individual words and ask him to read each word aloud. Then have him pick out the words that start with the same consonant sound or the same vowel sound. You might also have him search through magazines to find examples of his newly learned words.

4. Always try to proceed from the familiar to the unfamiliar, one step at a time. You might want to have the child utilize the following sequence: (a) learn names of actual objects, (b) associate the names with pictures of the objects, (c) demonstrate recognition of the words that name the pictured objects, and (d) finally demonstrate recognition of the printed words alone, without picture clues.

5. Whenever possible, plan and evaluate cooperatively with your students. Find out what *he* thinks his difficulty is, how he is trying to solve it, and what he would like to learn. Make the process of teaching and learning a mutual exercise in which both you and your students are working together to achieve a common goal. Remember that a youngster's feeling of involve-

ment and his sense of steady progress are extremely important to the successful outcome of his reading experiences.

SIGHT VOCABULARY WORDS

As you work with children, you will find that they learn some words by sight simply by memorizing them; words such as *though* would be difficult to learn in any other fashion. Moreover, it is obviously a great advantage to a youngster if he can recognize instantly more than half the words he comes across in his reading. Eventually, the skilled reader recognizes most words at sight and recognizes them so rapidly that he becomes almost oblivious to the process he uses to decode them because he knows the words so quickly and effortlessly.

While there are a variety of commercially produced vocabulary sight word lists, the most widely used is *The Dolch Word List* (Garrard Publishing Company: Champaign, Illinois). The *Dolch List* contains 220 words that make up from 50 to 75 percent of all school reading material. The first step in both the initial teaching of reading and in doing remedial work at a higher grade level is to see that each child can recognize these basic words instantly on sight.

Most teacher aides can easily learn how to use a word list in order to help children improve their reading skills. A sight word list is an enormously useful working tool. After it is mastered, it becomes a ready frame of reference from which to lead the child from the familiar ahead to the unfamiliar.

One of the simplest approaches for teaching basic sight words is to write the words on flash cards and use them with individual students who need additional vocabulary assistance. Hand the cards, a few at a time, to the child. Ask him to divide them into two piles; the first pile is the "known" words, and the second pile is the "unknown" words. When he has divided the words, have him read to you from the pile of "known" words. Put the "known" words in a file box where you and the child can enjoy watching the pile grow. Now you have an accurate frame of reference on which to base your teaching of new words.

Save the pile of "unknown" sight cards to work on later, to reintroduce and then review in quick drills or games. Most reading specialists recommend teaching no more than three unknown words at a time to slow learners and five to seven words at a time to a faster learner. Tell the child each unknown word and have him repeat it while looking at the word on the flash card. Then mix up the cards containing the unknown words and show them to the student once again, having him name the words as rapidly as he can. If needed, repeat the process until he knows all of the previously unknown words.

However, working only with flash cards soon becomes very dull. It is the process of reading itself that gives the student the most effective and pleasurable practice. Certainly, reading meaningful material is more interesting than merely calling words that have no relationship to each other. Oral reading is a quick and accurate way of appraising certain key reading skills such as word recognition and phrasing. It also can serve to identify specific words and word recognition skills where help is needed.

Word games help, too. You can play a quick game of tic-tac-toe using two sight words instead of *X* and *O*. Also, you can set up a bingo game by marking off a large card (the back of a spiral notebook will do) with five spaces across and five down and labeling the twenty-four spaces with words that the child needs practice on (the middle space is *FREE*). You will need a complete set of words plus several other words not on his board from which to draw. The covering markers (bottle caps work well) can be labeled with the same words that are on his board. He draws from the stack and then pronounces the words. The first child to make a pattern of a straight line, diagonal line, *X*, or *L*, wins.

You can even make up your own games with flash cards. Some possibilities are the following: (1) Each word the child pronounces quickly and correctly allows him to advance his marker around the bases of a baseball diamond or down a football field. (2) For each word, he answers correctly he is able to connect sequentially numbered dots on a connect-a-dot picture. (3) Divide twenty tokens between you: You give him a token for every word he gets right; he gives you a token for every word he misses. Whichever game you choose, play only while the child's interest and motivation are high. Ten or fifteen minutes for a game is usually a satisfactory time limit.

The sight word list is far more than just a tool for memorizing and reviewing words. It is also an important basis on which to build new words. By mastering the basic sight words, the student forms a familiar backdrop that helps him move to unfamiliar words in easy steps. Through repeated recognition of the same words in a variety of situations, the child gradually builds up his sight word vocabulary as he continues to mature in his reading.

STORYTELLING

There are many other techniques that can be utilized by teacher aides to contribute to an effective reading program. One of the more enjoyable techniques is that of storytelling, because almost all children like having adults tell them stories. There are an endless number of ways to tell stories. They can be read, acted out, illustrated with a flannel board, told with puppets, and so on.

Good storytelling, however, is a highly creative and an extremely personal experience. A special advantage of storytelling is that it is possible for both the storyteller and the listener to participate in a common experience. Together, they create a special world constructed with the words of the teller and the imagination of the listener. You, too, can construct this imaginary world with one or with sixty children, almost anywhere and at anytime, because the only props needed are your voice and the imagination of the listener.

However, before assuming the task of storytelling, you may want to take stock of yourself to determine what kinds of stories you tell most effectively. For example, if you do not feel at ease telling highly animated stories, steer away from those that require you to make loud noises or weird sounds. Perhaps you would better enjoy telling animal stories, mystery stories with complicated plots, or humorous stories. Regardless of the kind of story you select, it should be exciting enough to make you want to share the story with others.

Storytelling, as with any other art, improves with practice, and it is possible that you may need some help in perfecting your story-telling skills. For instance, you may need to learn to use your vocal tones to full capacity. This may be difficult to do in the beginning, for most of us are rather shy, but with experience you will become more of a "ham." In addition, you may need to practice using the full range of your voice, develop good breath control, and learn to project your voice properly. Emotions can be conveyed by your tone of voice. As you speak, it is possible for the inflection or the tone of your voice to change the meaning of a single word or an entire sentence.

You should also remember that you can create effective mental imagery with your words alone. Adjectives and adverbs are the words that create picturesque mental images in storytelling. Be sure to use descriptive words generously in your narrative. They not only help the child to visualize the story, but they appeal to his senses as well and expand his vocabulary as he hears unfamiliar words in a meaningful context.

You should not be surprised to learn that eye contact between the story-teller and listener is extremely important to an effective presentation. Successfully establishing good eye contact gives a youngster the feeling that the entire story is being told just for him. Also, eyes play another important function in storytelling. When two or more characters in a story are talking, you can help children keep track of who is saying what by moving your eyes back and forth, with each side representing a different character. Related to eye contact is body language. Potentially, your body language can be as effective in establishing mood, describing action, or in developing characters as the words you use to impart meaning. Proof of this can be found in the fact that a live rendition of a good story by a reasonably competent teacher aide holds the children's attention far longer than the same story on tape or record told by a master storyteller.

Finally, it is important to make any storytelling period a

relaxed, informal time in the classroom. The storyteller should be physically close to the children who are listening. Some aides like to gather the children around them, usually having them sit on the floor. Be sure to start each story session with at least some background setting for the story; include facts about all the characters in the story, and make any other preliminary comments necessary for better understanding and enjoyment of the story.

DIRECTING READING INTERESTS

Directing the reading interests of children along worthwhile lines and providing abundant material suitable for their reading is a continuing cooperative job shared by the classroom teacher, aide and librarian. For best results, resources of the home, school, and library should be pooled. The goal, of course, is to guide each child toward a balanced pattern of reading to help him discover and enjoy all the possibilities for entertainment and information that are to be found in good books.

Interest in reading is contagious. A teacher aide who is enthusiastic about reading and who enjoys many well-written children's books as well as adult books cannot help but convey her enthusiasm to youngsters. Such an aide calls the children's attention to new books when they arrive in the school library and, perhaps, reads aloud just enough of the story to arouse the children's interest. Such a procedure helps children find books they feel they will enjoy.

One of the most successful methods of converting a reluctant reader into an eager reader is to discover the subject in which he has a strong interest and then to supply him with a number of books that contain written information about his interests. Perhaps his interest is race cars. Track down all the books, magazines, and media materials you can find on the subject of race cars and drivers of race cars. More than likely, your reluctant reader will soon begin to see that there is at least one gratifying purpose in learning to read. Once you have interested him, he will be far more receptive to your efforts and be more cooperative as you attempt to teach him the skills he will need to master in order to read books in which he is interested.

There is no youngster in the world who does not want to learn to read well. The motivation is there — it needs only to be brought to the surface. Tutoring sessions offer a unique advantage in stimulating a child's motivation. Most school programs follow a set curriculum, regardless of the individual interests and needs of children. Through tutoring, this process can be reversed. The "curriculum" can be patterned and tailored to follow the individual interests of the child in order to fit his particular needs.

It will prove useful if you are familiar with the particular types of reading materials that children of various ages find especially enjoyable. While there are, of course, wide individual preferences, interests usually follow certain patterns. Children of five or six years of age usually prefer beautifully illustrated stories about animals, nature, or familiar everyday happenings. They also seem to enjoy jingles, riddles, simple poems, and rhymes. In the primary grades, children prefer stories that have the elements of surprise and interesting plots. Fairy tales are especially liked by youngsters in the second and third grades. In the intermediate grades (fourth, fifth, and sixth) boys seem to like "realistic" books and sport stories. Both boys and girls find appeal in biographies that are written in language easy to understand and in stories about other children and places, mystery stories, and animal stories.

When students are twelve or thirteen, they show greater interest in stories of adventure, excitement, mystery, humor, nature, and science fiction. As they grow older, boys and girls turn more to realistic stories of adventure. However, some girls may continue to favor themes of home life and begin to find their interests turning to romantic stories and sentimental fiction. Between the ages of thirteen and sixteen, both boys and girls seem to narrow their reading interests. Some boys especially like stories of sports and contests. Both boys and girls begin to broaden their reading interests to include history, historical fiction, biography, and travel stories. After the age of sixteen, young people's preferences begin to reflect their individualism and specialized interests still more. While older teens enjoy reading the same kinds of books that adults find pleasurable, they particularly enjoy literature related to their own interests and hobbies.

From time to time, ask yourself the following questions to help you evaluate your work in assisting and directing children's reading:

- Am I trying to identify and understand the varied needs and interests of the children I work with in the classroom?
- Am I encouraging children to read about the subjects that interest them?
- Am I providing reading materials that gradually increase in difficulty in order to encourage improvement and development of their reading skills?
- Am I cultivating good library habits in my students?
- Am I working with other resource people — teachers, librarians, parents — to provide a large variety of suitable reading materials?

ASSISTING CHILDREN IN THE LIBRARY

Independent reading activities should be considered one of the most important parts of any reading program. Suitable materials for supplemental reading should be provided and be readily accessible to students. A central library in a school with a well-trained, enthusiastic librarian in charge is an invaluable asset to any reading program. In addition, each classroom should have its own collection of at least fifty books, varying widely in difficulty, content, and style. Time for independent reading should be built into every teacher's classroom schedule, because supplemental reading provides children the chance to read in a highly individualized way. Each child can set his own pace, select his own reading material, follow his own interests, sample a varied assortment of literature, and proceed at his own pace.

Whether your school has individual classroom libraries or maintains a central library, you can be a strong asset to your school's reading program by teaching library skills to children. For example, youngsters need to learn how to use the card catalog in locating books and materials on the library shelves. Children need opportunities to practice locating information in card catalogs; encourage them to seek your help when they become puzzled or confused. You can show children how to use the card catalog to answer the following questions about every book in the library:

- Where will I find a book with this title?
- How can I find a book if I know only the author's name?
- Where in the library can I find books in certain specialized fields?
- What books does the library have on this subject? Where will I find these books?

There are also many other kinds of reference materials with which youngsters should become acquainted before they finish elementary school. These resource materials include encyclopedias, almanacs, yearbooks, atlases, biographic dictionaries, and a thesaurus, etc. If possible, youngsters should examine and compare several different kinds of each one of these basic research tools. An introduction to these resources by a teacher or aide can open up new avenues for independent learning. The teaching sequence of skills essential for locating information includes (1) learning what types of information can be found in various reference works; (2) deciding under which headings or entries the information is likely to be found; and (3) locating the correct volume in works of more than one volume.

In addition to the general kinds of duties you may be asked to perform, your duties in regard to library activities may also include:

1. Handling basic book circulation routines — checking cards, renewing, or checking out books.
2. Assisting students in locating reference materials.
3. Mending and repairing torn books and magazines.
4. Helping to set up audiovisual equipment for individual listening or viewing.
5. Designing appealing bulletin boards for the library.

6. Reviewing monthly periodicals and bulletins for items of interest to teachers.
7. Adding to the picture file by cutting, mounting, and classifying pictures from old magazines.
8. Making bibliographies when teachers request them; putting books on reserve for teachers.

THE TEACHER AIDE'S ROLE

An alert teacher aide can use each reading activity as an opportunity to get better acquainted with the reading performance levels of the children in her classroom. For example, you can assist the teacher in discovering youngsters who are following the words with their fingers, holding their books too closely, using poor reading posture, or moving their lips while reading silently. In addition, particular strengths and weaknesses regarding comprehension and word-attack skills can be observed and noted when children answer questions orally and in writing about their reading material.

Even though commercially prepared reading materials are attractive, convenient methods of instruction, there are many times when these materials are simply not available to you due to their comparatively high cost. However, creative teacher aides can use simple techniques to construct materials and activities that effectively supplement and enrich the school's reading program. These supplementary reading activities include word games, skill charts, hand puppets, flannelboard characters, and practice worksheets, etc. Each activity should be accompanied by a written purpose and skill development objective. In addition, each activity should be simple, attractive, and durable if it is to be used more than once. Magazines, newspapers, old workbooks, and coloring books can be highly useful, constructive resource materials.

Some further suggestions for ways you can help children acquire needed reading skills are listed. These activities can be used in either game form or simply as skill exercises:

1. Help children construct three-dimensional models — on table-tops, and sandboxes, etc. — that depict scenes or

characters from stories they have enjoyed reading.

2. Construct mobiles of storybook characters; use simple materials such as clothes hangers and cardboard cutouts.
3. Help children use the flannelboard cutouts they have made to tell part of a story or to depict the action described as they read a selected portion from a book out loud to the class.
4. Let one child pantomime or act out silently a part of a story that he has just read.
5. Help children to write poems and rhymes that express or paraphrase a story they have read.
6. Display a collection of mounted pictures; ask the children to write a descriptive story explaining or identifying each picture.
7. Cut up a short story from a children's magazine into sections and mount the parts on tagboard. After the parts are scrambled, the children can be asked to number the sections of the story in proper order according to the action sequence.

SUMMARY

You have probably already discovered that more teachers use aides in the area of reading instruction than in any other academic area within the school curriculum. In large part, this is due to the fact that children learn to read in a vast variety of ways; therefore, reading instruction demands that adequate attention be given to individualized learning instruction. Likewise, there are a variety of effective techniques for teaching children the basic skills in reading, but underlying each of these techniques is the common need for well-planned, sequentially developed instruction. The statements above reveal but a few of the reasons why you play such a vital role in your school's reading program.

While learning to read, children are also learning to like reading — or to dislike it. They are constantly forming either positive or negative attitudes toward reading. They are either learning to think of reading as fun and something they like to do, or they are learning to look upon reading as something distasteful and a requirement to be gotten through as rapidly as possible. By working cooperatively with your supervising teacher, you can help make reading a pleasant experience for children. You can help guide each child toward a balanced pattern of reading where he will discover the enjoyment, adventure, and knowledge that awaits him in the world of books.

CHAPTER 7

ASSISTING WITH OTHER SUBJECTS

WHETHER assisting children with homework, tutoring, or helping a child select a library book, the aim of the teacher aide remains the same. No matter what the subject is, your primary goal should be to provide a supportive atmosphere to youngsters who are long on failure and short on self-confidence.

Most of the general ideas and many of the specific activities already suggested in the chapter regarding reading instruction are usable either in their entirety or with some adaptation when you assist with other curriculum areas. Since the child's performance in all subjects depends primarily upon his ability to read, teacher aides working with students in all curriculum areas may well find themselves involved in developing reading skills. Yet, most aides find a need for improving the specialized techniques they use when working in a variety of subject areas.

Teacher aides can find rewarding opportunities throughout the full range of subject areas. For example, an extra set of hands is always welcome when it comes to giving children experience in art; an extra pair of eyes to help supervise cleanup time is a real help, too. Sometimes a teacher is fortunate in finding that her aide is an accomplished piano player. However, even if your classroom is without the benefit of a piano player, one thing is certain; every aide can learn to operate a tape recorder or a record player to enable the children to sing along with recorded music. Also, keep in mind that learning a few chords on the Autoharp® takes but a few minutes, and many songbooks have Autoharp chords indicated above the melody line of each song. In addition, an aide may have had extensive experience in directing physical education activities and will therefore enjoy strengthening the school's instruction in this area of the curriculum. Maybe your expertise lies in other subject areas of the curriculum, such as new math, social studies, or science. At any rate, you will find greater job satisfaction and improved personal relationships if you make known your special interests and/or talents to the administrators who place teacher aides in their job assignments.

HELPING WITH MATHEMATICS

Classroom teachers report that next to reading instruction, students need more individualized help in mathematics than in any other subject. However, for many children, before any significant success can be attained in mathematics, they must overcome a genuine fear of the subject. At this point, you can be the individual who successfully assists a youngster in conquering his fear, while at the same time you are strengthening his ability to compute with greater accuracy. You can help him achieve and maintain a cycle of success, for as he grows more confident in his ability, his performance will undoubtedly improve; as his performance level continues to improve, he continues to gain greater confidence and increased motivation to continue.

If you are to be of assistance in helping children with mathematics, you should be aware of some important changes that have occurred in today's mathematics curriculum. First, current emphasis rests more on *meaning* than on simple memorization of math facts. Children are now being taught *why* as well as *how*. They are given an opportunity to explore and discover in the hope and expectation that out of these explorations comes meaning. Second, certain key mathematical processes are now introduced earlier in the school curriculum. For example, kindergarten youngsters study basic geometric concepts. They learn that a figure that has three sides is called a triangle. Likewise, math concepts that once were found only in the junior and senior high school curriculum have now been moved down into the elementary grades. A third important change in the mathematics curriculum is the fact that the subject is now called *mathematics* instead of arithmetic. This means that children learn that the operations they perform are governed by specific mathematical laws.

Take heart, however, because the new math is not really so

very different from the arithmetic of earlier years, except, of course, that now there is as much emphasis on *why* things are so as there is on *how* they work. Besides simply learning how to add a column of figures, youngsters nowadays are taught *why* the answer is written in a particular way or *why* the same answer would be possible if arrived at in a different way.

You will find that tutoring students in mathematics often calls for using the same basic techniques discussed in the previous chapter on reading. However, in math instruction, it is even more important than in reading instruction to have short and varied lessons. When math is discussed, many students' attention spans are extremely short. In order to keep students' interest alive and active, the learning activities must be varied. Most successful and efficient math sessions are short presentations of a math concept followed by brief periods of independent practice work. The written exercises assigned to students must be brief. Prolonged periods of unsupervised written work usually result in having the students merely practice errors repeatedly.

Probably you have heard adults make statements such as, "I don't even know enough about the subject to ask an intelligent question"; remember that formulating questions is an essential part of the learning process, and it is a skill that can be developed only through practice. When helping with the subject of mathematics, give youngsters as many opportunities as possible to stop you and ask questions while you are explaining a certain process. The answer to a child's particular question may be exactly the information he needs to fill in a learning gap and make the entire concept clear. Also, he is probably asking a question that other children in the class are wondering about. No question or answer should be considered "dumb" or trivial in the learning process. In fact, you will find that children's questions give you excellent clues to the kinds of problems the entire class may be having. Develop your ability to listen for these clues.

TEACHING MATH SKILLS

Many children have difficulty with math, because beyond a

certain point, they don't see that it is useful in their everyday lives. You can help to instill a greater interest in the subject of mathematics by demonstrating various ways it is useful to the youngsters. For instance, capitalize on most boys' interest in sports by having them turn to the sports section of a daily newspaper and work out each baseball player's batting average for his performance the previous day, or, bring a road map to class and plan an automobile trip. Find out how far the proposed destination is; find out how much the gasoline will cost if the car gets 15 miles to the gallon; find out how long it will take to get there if you drive an average of 55 miles per hour.

Use "real world" situations as resource material for your teaching of mathematics. Younger children especially profit from manipulating tangible objects such as buttons and beans when learning a mathematical process. When working with older children, give them a newspaper ad or catalog and let them simulate the process of spending exactly fifty dollars. Likewise, let the children use supermarket ads from the local newspaper to develop and solve problems using mathematical skills in such basic processes as addition, subtraction, multiplication, fractions, and percentages, etc.

Aides as well as teachers are always looking for new ways to take the drudgery out of math drill activities. Asking children to learn tables of math facts hardly contributes to making learning mathematics a pleasurable experience. Therefore, here are some simple but effective suggestions you might want to use the next time you assist in teaching mathematics.

FRACTION FUN. Cut out small squares of paper or cardboard; on each square write a fraction you want the children to master. Then on the chalkboard write the percentage equivalent for the fraction on the square. Scramble the squares of paper in a hat or box and have each student pick one square and match it with the percentage equivalent on the chalkboard. If the student matches the percentage equivalent correctly, he receives one point. If his match is incorrect, he gets only a fraction of a point — the same fraction he missed. The winner of the game is the student who has amassed the most points at the end of the game.

GUESS THE PRICE. Play this game to teach concepts about money. All you need is an old catalog with the prices blocked out. Once the students have learned how to evaluate the costs of items, they then estimate the prices of other similar items. The youngster whose estimate is closest to the actual price listed in the catalog wins the game.

ZIP-ZAP-ZOOP. Begin the game by having the children line up. On the chalkboard write *zip-zap-zoop*, and under each word write a digit; for example, you want to write 4 under zip, 6 under zap, and 7 under zoop. Beginning at one end of the line, ask the children to count off. When the count reaches a number which is a multiple of the digit listed below zip, zap, or zoop, the youngster should say the corresponding word in place of the number. For instance, with 4, 6, 7 as zip, zap, and zoop, you would count, "1, 2, 3, zip, 5, zap, zoop, zip, 9, 10, 11," and so on. A number such as 12, which is a multiple of both 4 and 6 would be zip-zap, and a number such as 84, which is a multiple of all three, would be zip-zap-zoop.

DRILL DAYS. Some days could be set aside as drill days to emphasize, for example, a certain multiplication fact. "Today is 7 × 6 day" you might announce in the morning. During the day, children can tap anybody (students and adults) on the back and ask them for the answer to 7 × 6.

GIVE ME YOUR NUMBER. Form two teams (A and B) of ten students each. Each one of the ten team members wears a large cardboard number indicating different numbers from 0 to 9. You say, "Team A, give me a 41," members of Team A wearing 4 and 1 form 41. If they should form 14 instead or some other incorrect number, Team B gets a chance to try. You can make the game more difficult by asking the children to form the answers to simple addition, subtraction, or multiplication problems.

LANGUAGE ARTS

In addition to the subject of reading, language arts instruction includes the other subject areas of spelling, language usage, and handwriting. All of these skill areas are used constantly, because they are essential to the mastery of all the other subject areas found in today's school curriculum.

There are specific skills involved in the teaching of language arts that require your special attention. Generally speaking, your work is with underachievers. Children who have difficulty in reading often have similar problems in language usage, spelling, and handwriting. As you tutor children in reading, you can also help them to improve their performance in other important related subject areas. For example, when a youngster learns to read a new word, you can provide him with an opportunity to write the new word as well as to learn how to spell it correctly. You might want to employ stories, games, or the chalkboard to achieve this goal. The act of writing reinforces his reading skills in addition to his spelling and handwriting skills, and if he is writing the words in a story that he has created himself, you are also reinforcing the skills used in written expression.

You can also assist the classroom teacher in developing spelling word lists for children who need individual help. It would be helpful to write the words down for the student and perhaps work with him each day on special activities that help him to learn his spelling words. In addition, when a certain group of students is assigned a specific list of spelling words, you can be of valuable assistance by helping the group with their assigned supplemental spelling exercises by calling out the words during the spelling test, by correcting the test papers, and by entering the students' grades in the teacher's gradebook.

A teacher aide can also work with students on the so-called spelling demons. Since these difficult and tricky words often do not conform to accepted spelling rules, sound the way they look, or look the way they sound, untold hazards abound for the unwary speller. Such words as *seize, surprise,* and *rhythm* are good examples of the English language's inconsistencies. Place some of these "spelling demons" on visual-aid charts and work on them with small groups of students to help the children remember the difficult spellings of these "demons" that are exceptions to the spelling rules they have learned.

Regardless of the fact that the mass media is burgeoning with ever more diverse methods of mass communication, handwriting remains the basic means of communication. There are two points to keep in mind when working with students to improve their penmanship. First, children should be able to write legibly. Legibility is the prime prerequisite for understanding. Second, students must be shown the proper way to sit as well as the proper way to hold their pens or pencils, so that they will be able to write for long periods of time without undue discomfort. Simply put, the best way for children to master penmanship is to practice. A few minutes practice a day produces surprisingly good results.

You should keep in mind that the chalkboard is an excellent resource for children who have occasional difficulty with specific letters, as well as for those who have persistent handwriting problems. The teacher or aide can observe fairly closely a group of students who are practicing their handwriting simultaneously at the chalkboard. In addition, it is much easier for you to guide a child's hand through the motions necessary to create a letter at the board. Besides, children love to write on the chalkboard; therefore, motivation is automatically created for an activity that is normally one of the less exciting events in the day for children.

To illustrate a typical case of how you can assist with language arts instruction, examine the case of an elementary school teacher who has been working with her class of fourth graders on language usage. The teacher selects a small group of students for diagnosis while you assist the remainder of the class as they work on nouns. She may discover that four or five students are having difficulty using singular and plural nouns correctly. When she has diagnosed a common deficiency in a certain group of students, she can call you over to the group and give you specific instructions regarding remedial activities to perform with these students.

At this point, you can reinforce what the classroom teacher

has already begun with the students. In the example of the language class, the reinforcement may simply be a matter of giving the children further practice in identifying singular and plural nouns. You can work closely with the students in a natural teaching situation. By helping students determine the number of persons, places, or objects to which a certain noun refers, you can assist the children in answering questions about whether a particular noun is singular or plural.

SCIENCE ACTIVITIES

Almost all children wonder about the world in which they live and are curious to find out more about it. Such curiosity is the natural gift children bring to the science class, and you need only to build on it. When a youngster questions why something is so or why it works as it does, your best answer is, "Let's find out."

In addition to contributing to the general objective of furthering the child's education, science instruction also has specific objectives. These objectives include helping the child to understand basic scientific facts, concepts, and principles; enabling the child to use problem-solving skills; developing scientific attitudes such as open-mindedness; generating the ability to describe the benefits and limitations of science; and developing a genuine appreciation for and interest in science. The teaching of science should involve youngsters in creative activities, suggest science-related leisure-time pursuits, and make all children more aware of the opportunities for employment in scientific fields.

The kind of help you give students in science depends upon several factors: the area of science being pursued; your own scientific knowledge, background, and interest; the child's specific difficulties or facilities in the area of science; and the quality and quantity of the school's equipment and facilities for carrying out scientific experimentation. However, even though a teacher aide usually has neither the academic background to conduct complicated scientific experiments nor the sophisticated laboratories necessary for the experiments, with a few simple, easily accessible materials she can open up the world of science to her youngsters. For example, by purchasing a package of flower seeds, she can reap exciting benefits in her classroom science instruction. Or, with an inexpensive magnet and various common household objects, students can be taught the basic principles of magnetism.

Even the least scientifically inclined aide has had some basic experiences that are useful in science. A rock or shell collector has an immediate resource with which to seize the interests of students. An experienced gardener has a wealth of scientific information that can be shared with a group of eager youngsters. Perhaps an aide has a butterfly collection and would be willing to show it or to present slides of her specimens.

Further, in order to promote the development of the scientific process, stimulating questions are of vital necessity. Teachers need to ask questions to find out what students know and what they don't know, to arouse interest, to evaluate student progress, to review, and to summarize. The following specific techniques for improving your questioning skills should prove useful as you assist teachers with science instruction:

1. Ask questions as simply, concisely, and directly as possible.
2. Ask the question before designating which child should answer.
3. Ask questions of as many children as possible during a science lesson.
4. Ask questions that are specific rather than too broad or general.
5. Ask as many questions as possible that will stimulate the children's creative and divergent thinking processes.
6. Avoid repeating children's answers to questions except when the answers cannot be heard.

SOCIAL STUDIES TECHNIQUES

As you work with children in social studies, you will often hear the term *the inquiry method.* The inquiry process is a pattern of related activities designed to stimulate and encourage investigation and to create the desire to seek additional information. This method is rather like what educators have long called *problem-solving techniques*. An example of the inquiry approach was observed by the authors recently in a fourth grade teacher's classroom. The children were studying the American colonial period, and the teacher was attempting to get across the idea that the colonists were forced to undergo many hardships in order to have even the daily necessities of life. The teacher could have simply told them this, but instead she suggested that the students make hand-dipped candles. By the time the children had completed this tedious chore, they had formed a much clearer idea of at least one hardship that the colonists faced. The more learning is related to the child's own experiences and the more he is encouraged to question and investigate, the more genuine and lasting is his learning. This is what the "new social studies" is trying to tell us. Yet, the inquiry method is not an easy way to teach. It requires a great deal of teaching skill as well as a great deal of assistance from the teacher aide.

If the inquiry method of teaching social studies is to be truly successful, teachers need to provide individual students with opportunities to study and work apart from the entire group. Not only do youngsters need to develop responsibility for their own learning, but they also need to encounter challenges that bring forth intellectual inquiry and creativity. Conventional group assignments in social studies that result in the traditional routine of classroom studies inevitably deny students their best opportunities for independent study and investigation.

When using the independent study technique in social studies as well as in other subject areas, keep in mind that you must know your subject matter well enough to answer the children's questions confidently and intelligently. Throughout the independent study process, you will be expected to assume the following kinds of responsibilities:

1. Circulating in the classroom to see if children are completing their work.
2. Working on specific skills with individual students.

3. Providing emotional support and close supervision for children exhibiting behavior problems.
4. Giving, repeating, or explaining teacher-prepared instructions.
5. Assisting students who are looking up information.

ART AND MUSIC

No one who has seen the delight on a child's face when he is in the process of creating something can deny the value of art and music activities in the growth and development of children. One of the most effective vehicles for a child's creative expression is art. This form of creative expression may be a major influence in the child's success in identifying and developing the creative resources he has within himself. It is impossible for a drawing to be "wrong" if it expresses the child's inner feelings about a special subject or event. Similarly, musical expression provides a valuable outlet for ideas and feelings the child can express no other way.

Teacher aides serving in art instruction classes can perform many important preparation and postclass tasks. The results of these tasks can be transformed directly into extra minutes or even hours during the school day for the busy classroom or art teacher. Of course, there are many other services an aide can perform in the field of art instruction. Since there never seems to be enough space in the classroom to do the big art projects that are always so much fun for the children, you could alleviate the space problem by supervising a small group working in an out-of-the-way spot located in some other part of the school building. You could also supervise children who are arranging a display of their work in a showcase or on a bulletin board.

An aide in the art classroom can make it easier for the teacher to get a number of projects going at the same time. With your help in providing additional direction and supervision, small groups can function much more effectively and efficiently. Likewise, collecting art ideas from professional magazines such as *Teacher* or *Instructor* or from available art publications would be a good project for a teacher aide. Professional magazines can usually be found in the school's library. These ideas could then be classified and filed according to their appropriate grade levels, degree of difficulty, or subject areas. Your finished product is a valuable resource file of easy-to-do projects that the whole class can use.

When working with children in art, you can make their art experiences more meaningful if you keep in mind the following do's and don'ts.

Do's

1. Do discuss topics that lend themselves to artistic expression.
2. Do help children find subjects to draw that are important to them.
3. Do be generous but judicious with your praise.
4. Do provide a variety of types of creative opportunities.
5. Do discuss the children's finished art projects with them.

Don'ts

1. Don't correct the child's artwork unless the child himself is dissatisfied with it and asks for suggestions.
2. Don't stress competition.
3. Don't ask children to draw objects as they appear to you.
4. Don't substitute coloring books, cutouts, or mimeographed drawings for true art experiences.

Ordinarily, the teacher aide who helps with music has both interest and experience in this area. However, the lack of musical ability is not necessarily an overwhelming handicap except, perhaps, when dealing with a child who is unusually musically talented. An aide can, for instance, help in the selection of the music and the form in which it is to be presented. Dance and sing-along records are always popular with children of all ages.

Many dances that are taught to children by the teacher can be made more enjoyable by a teacher aide who assists with supervision. As you provide additional help, you may be involved in distributing materials, carrying out the teacher's assignments with small groups, or helping youngsters create their own movements. An aide does not need a great deal of musical talent or musical background to be successful. What she does need, of course, is the desire to help children and the required patience to carry out the assigned tasks.

Music instruction does not have to be limited to the classroom. Effective lessons can be carried on in the gym or even on the playground. A record player and an extra-long extension cord can turn a playground into a music area where children can let their creativity flow. A teacher aide can often provide the essential, timely assistance that provides richer music experience for children.

PHYSICAL EDUCATION DUTIES

The process of education today is concerned with the total growth and development of the child. Physical education is an integral part of that process; it contributes to the psychomotor, cognitive, and affective development of the youngsters. It serves the divergent needs of all children — the slow learner, the minority group member, the handicapped, the gifted — and is geared to the developmental needs of each child.

As a physical education aide, you can give the instructor much more time for teaching by taking care of such routine chores as taking attendance, keeping records, charting the children's progress, maintaining and distributing equipment, and administering written and performance skill tests. In addition, if you have specialized knowledge and skill in an area where the teacher has only a general background knowledge, you may prove to be especially beneficial to the class by introducing the children to a whole new range of physical education experiences they would not have been exposed to otherwise.

As an aide, you may be asked to take charge of small group instruction while the physical education teachers works with the larger group, or you may be asked to supervise the larger group while the teacher gives individualized instruction. Also, you may be asked to serve as a demonstrator or safety assistant when the class is using equipment that requires additional supervision, such as when using a trampoline.

Generally speaking, aides in physical education release certified teachers from their routine, nonspecialized duties and responsibilities that heretofore have prevented them from developing a full schedule of activities for the children. Physical education aides often perform the following kinds of services:

1. Assist in the care and maintenance of equipment
2. Handle clerical work, including care of inventories and requisition forms
3. Keep growth and development charts and other types of individual and group records for diagnosis
4. Assist teachers with individual and group workouts and practice sessions
5. Supervise locker rooms, shower areas, and playgrounds

Basic first aid training is an absolute must for the teacher aide who supervises children in physical education, whether in a formal physical education class or on the playground. In addition, first aid supplies should be easily accessible in high-risk areas, and teacher aides should be familiar with their location as well as how and when to use them.

SUMMARY

A teacher aide can be of service in areas beyond as well as within the classroom. She can assist with activities and projects in art, music, and physical education. She can serve as a tutor in mathematics, work with audiovisual equipment in social studies, or supervise seatwork in science. As a teacher aide, you will be encouraged to participate in as many classroom activities as possible. In the classroom, you are not only helping the teacher to do her job more effectively, you are also in a position to learn by doing and thus gain greater experience and insight into the teacher-learning process.

The success you experience as a classroom aide depends in large measure on your ability to establish a meaningful working relationship with the teacher. It is her responsibility to determine the structure and direction of the instruction so that it will be of the greatest benefit for the class. It is your responsibility to assist her in carrying out that instruction. You must constantly communicate with the teacher in regard to information that has been learned that is relevant to future instructional decisions. However, it is imperative that you recognize that instructional decisions are to be made only by the classroom teacher.

CHAPTER 8

UTILIZING MULTIMEDIA MATERIALS

ONE of the most important developments in modern education is the growing use of multimedia audiovisual aids for instruction. Since almost 85 percent of what is learned begins through the visual and auditory senses, it is only natural that educators should appeal to children's minds chiefly through sight and sound. The chief objective of this chapter is to help teacher aides learn how to prepare and utilize audiovisual aids in the classroom.

It cannot be overemphasized that the effective use of multimedia aids in learning requires skill on the part of both teachers and teacher aides. The effective instructor uses appropriate audiovisual aids at the proper time and in the proper way to personalize her multimedia instruction. However, such aids should be regarded only as aids. Multimedia materials are not intended to replace effective instructional techniques already being used. They are most effective when they are utilized to supplement the teaching skill of the instructor and to assist in student assimilation and application. Instructional methods that combine appropriate audiovisual materials, well-written textbooks, and effective teaching techniques create an ideal learning situation.

Multimedia instruction has demonstrated its importance in the teaching-learning process. Yet, many teachers who feel they lack preparation in specific skills needed to utilize multimedia materials and equipment have been driven by feelings of insecurity to shy away from using available materials. Teacher aides who become familiar with the operation and potential use of media equipment and materials can often bring a much-needed skill to the classroom.

THE VALUE OF MULTIMEDIA MATERIALS

The use of multimedia materials can vitalize an entire

teaching session; one film or filmstrip can help make a lesson topic remain vividly in the memories of your students. Audiovisual aids can serve as substitutes for firsthand experiences while also enhancing the students' verbal understanding. Used as such, they are not frills but an integral part of the learning process. Therefore, some of the practical values of multimedia resourses are sketched.

First, the materials provide a means for overcoming many limitations that often plague students who have had restricted personal experiences. Opportunities for valuable personal experiences are often limited for individuals and in their local communities. More than any other teaching technique, audiovisual presentations tend to provide a way of equalizing background experiences for every child. If students cannot be taken to cultural events or historical places, then the events and places can be brought to them and experienced vicariously.

Second, media overcomes the limitations of the classroom. Obviously, it may be difficult or impossible to experience some events within the classroom. For instance, a trip to New York, although exceedingly valuable, may still leave many learning experiences untouched due to the enormity of the undertaking. Therefore, a good thirty-minute film might conceivably be much more effective and do a more thorough teaching job than the actual experience. On the other hand, some objects or organisms are too small to be observed without mechanical aids. Protozoa and bacteria must be studied under magnification. Slides and films are extremely beneficial to classes studying these subjects. Other phenomena may be too slow or even too fast to be seen and studied with the unaided eye. Time-lapse and slow-motion photography can be utilized effectively to show some types of subjects or events. Many topics are too complex to examine without the aid of audiovisual materials. For example, animated diagrams help simplify complex structures and phenomena.

Third, media provides uniformity of perceptual experiences. As an individual perceives, his reactions and conclusions depend partly on stimuli and partly on his background experiences, which are used to provide meaning. Audiovisual materials provide all children with common perceptual experiences. A projected magnification of the wings of a butterfly enables each student to see clearly what the teacher wishes the class to see, but under a microscope some students may miss the essential points altogether.

Fourth, audiovisual aids provide initial concepts that are correct, real, and complete. Learning things correctly the first time is economical learning. Errors and misinformation must be followed by diagnostic study and remedial treatment. It is much easier to learn the correct subtraction combinations initially than to learn them incorrectly and later have to make corrections. Often, an instructor has difficulty explaining a process, with the result that different students get different and often erroneous conceptions of the topic being discussed. Pictures, models, graphs, films, and similar instructional materials are among the best means of providing the correct information when introducing a new concept.

Fifth, media materials awaken new desires and interests in students. As youngsters' experiences are broadened and enriched, their perceptions become more complete, and they inevitably respond with new desires, attitudes, and interests. Such changes are usually translated into positive gains, such as increased reading skills, better problem-solving skills, and a heightened appreciation for new and different experiences.

Sixth, audiovisual aids provide motivation and stimulation for learning. When an instructor is about to begin a new unit on proper health practices, he may wish to provide the proper stimulation for getting a maximum effort from his students. A few well-selected pictures for the bulletin board may help, or a short film or demonstration may prove useful. These materials are equally effective in renewing interest as the unit develops. Audiovisual materials have an important psychological effect on stimulating student interest.

Finally, media can provide integrated experiences varying from the concrete to the abstract. Few, if any, other teaching materials or techniques have the versatility of multimedia materials. Their diversity provides for all kinds of individual variations in the learners' abilities and includes many types of experiences from concrete to abstract. For example, a good film on the Lincoln Memorial presents concrete images of the size, location, and appearance of the monument and may also encourage the students to make generalizations about the meaning of liberty and other far-reaching abstractions.

HOW TO USE MULTIMEDIA MATERIALS

Depending in large measure upon her assignment, a teacher aide may be called upon to use many kinds of multimedia or audiovisual aids. Regardless of whether you work in a kindergarten classroom, in a media center, or in a clerical capacity, you will at one time or another be involved in ordering, presenting, or operating audiovisual aids.

While each multimedia presentation is a unique experience, the following suggestions may prove useful in using audiovisual materials:

1. Learn about the kinds of media materials and equipment that are available in your school. Ask the media director or your librarian for a list or catalog.
2. Familiarize yourself with these media materials and equipment.
3. Learn how to operate the equipment you plan to use.
4. Always preview materials and evaluate them for suitability.
5. Set up the equipment before the class begins and before the students come into the room for the media presentation.
6. Avoid using too many different types of media materials during a single class period.
7. Return the equipment and materials to the proper storage area when finished; report all defective equipment and materials promptly.

Since using media materials is not quite as simple as opening a textbook, it is important to know some basic procedures to follow. Without question, proper operation of multimedia equipment can make or break a particular presentation. Not having the equipment ready on time, fumbling its operation, or causing breakdowns by mishandling can completely destroy the effectiveness of media presentations.

The best way to ensure a good working knowledge of equipment is to reserve some practice time with it. Obviously, it takes a certain amount of expertise to thread and rewind a film projector or to operate a tape recorder efficiently. If it is at all possible, make sure you schedule some practice sessions with someone who possesses adequate knowledge of the equipment. A mistake made in a practice session is one less mistake to be performed in the classroom before a group of restless children.

Last-minute disturbances and hurried presentations are detrimental to an effective media program. Many problems can be avoided if the following steps are taken:

1. *Preview media materials.* This is a must in order to insure proper handling of media materials. For future reference, it is also advisable to note briefly the content of the material on file cards, including the title, running time, type, and source. After the initial preview, it is necessary only to check the file before utilizing that particular media aid. Often, an instructor's manual or guide is included with audiovisual materials.

2. *Set up equipment and screen.* In most cases, it is necessary to set up some type of equipment in order to use media aids. For example, if a film projector is going to be used, be sure that the distance between the projector and the screen makes easy viewing possible for the students. In order to provide the best viewing conditions, the screen should be placed so that the bottom is approximately at the eye level of the seated students.

3. *Check seating arrangement.* Most films, filmstrips, and overhead transparencies viewed outside of a 60° angle become distorted; therefore, it is advisable to place all seats within the confines of this space. If seats are permanently attached, ask students not to use the seats outside this area. Also avoid using chairs directly in front of the screen.

4. *Check lighting.* Except when using an overhead projector, it is almost always necessary to darken the room. If it is neces-

sary for students to take notes on the media presentation, use the classroom lights instead of raising the window shades. Try to prevent light rays from shining directly onto the screen or in students' faces.

5. *Check ventilation.* A hot, stuffy, dark room induces drowsiness. Often, it is wise to sacrifice complete darkness to avoid poor ventilation. Room temperatures over 72° or humidity above 50 percent dulls alertness and adversely affects learning.

PRESENTING MULTIMEDIA MATERIALS

An otherwise excellent teaching aid may be worthless if it is not presented properly. A good instructor lays a strong foundation for learning and arouses student enthusiasm by effectively using media materials. The following procedures should prove useful to inexperienced as well as experienced aides in presenting multimedia materials.

1. *Introductory remarks.* Put the class at ease with a few carefully chosen remarks. Then, in a simple, straightforward manner identify the subject matter of the audiovisual presentation. Your introductory remarks should make the students want to learn. Focus the students' attention on important highlights to be seen during the presentation.

2. *Presentation.* Retention of learned material is almost doubled when a class is properly prepared for an audiovisual presentation. Students should know why the material is being used and what to look for. Particularly, students should be alerted to unfamiliar or new words, charts, or other illustrations occurring in the material.

The film or other type of media selected should be shown as a part of the normal process of instruction. Audiovisual materials must be vehicles for learning, not just displays.

3. *Apply instruction.* Apply the information immediately to specific problems or instructional activities. A good discussion helps students to internalize and assimilate information contained in the media presentation. You might wish to select one student to explain procedures, facts, information, skills, or attitudes to the group. "Learning by doing" through student dem-

onstrations and active group participation has proven to be a highly effective teaching technique.

4. *Test students.* The students' understanding of the lesson should be thoroughly tested by the instructor. The test can be oral or written, but it should be brief, specific, and to the point.

HOW'S YOUR MQ*

Score one point for each *Yes*

1. Do you utilize media material in a regular classroom setting, avoiding large group presentations (two or more classes together)?_____

2. Do you utilize only media materials that serve the needs of your students and are pertinent to current instructional objectives?_____

3. Do you always preview the media presentation prior to using it with your entire class?_____

4. Do you introduce the film to your class – indicating points to look for and explaining difficult words used in the film?_____

5. Do you operate all media equipment carefully in order to avoid damage?_____

6. Do you make it a point to never leave any media equipment while it is running?_____

7. Do you always have films threaded and the title in focus prior to your introductory remarks?_____

8. Do you know where to locate replacement parts for media equipment in your building? _____

9. Do you allow sufficient time for class discussion of information contained in the media presentation?_____

10. Do you immediately return all media equipment and materials to their proper location?_____

How Do You Rate:

10 points = Professional
 9 points = Definitely gifted
 8 points = Capable
 7 points = Inconclusive
 6 points
 or less   = Hide your score

_____

* Media Quotient

Objective tests of the true-false, multiple-choice, matching, or completion type have the edge over the more cumbersome and lengthy subjective discussion examination.

5. *Review the lesson.* All errors discovered during the testing process should be corrected and retaught. The instructor should not hesitate to reshow the media presentation. Remember, if the student has not learned — the instructor has not taught.

HOW TO USE FILMSTRIPS

In many teaching situations, the filmstrip is considered the most valuable audiovisual teaching aid. One advantage of filmstrips over motion-picture films is that each frame on a filmstrip can be readily projected on the screen for any length of time. The students and instructor can then discuss the film's contents in as great detail as may be required by the rate of learning desired.

Not all subjects need to be portrayed in motion to be properly understood. The architecture of a fine European castle or the outline of an island, for example, can be presented better by using projected still pictures than by using a film. When motion is not an important characteristic of the subject, a filmstrip is an effective instructional device.

Filmstrips offer a wide coverage of subject matter. The production of filmstrips has reached a point where excellent materials are available for all levels, from primary grades to college. The quality of the materials has been so constantly improved that their artwork and photography are representative of the best in the graphic arts.

At what point in the teaching process should filmstrips be used? The answer depends upon the type of lesson or unit being presented and the specific objectives involved. A third-grade teacher suggests one point where a filmstrip is especially advantageous: "Do you want a simple and easy, yet interesting and worthwhile, motivation for a science unit? If so, try a filmstrip." Numerous other ways to use filmstrips can be cited:

• *Introduction of a unit* stimulates interest in a unit.

- *Appreciation lesson* provides background in art, literature, history, fairy tales, and all kinds of fantasy.
- *Group discussion* provokes comments: Students like to discuss the pictures they have seen; with the filmstrip, the pictures can be discussed frame by frame.
- *Drill lesson* furnishes a new approach to drill work, helps sustain interest, and adds variety.
- *Review lesson* provides for an interesting method of drawing conclusions and adds enrichment.

UTILIZING OPAQUE AND OVERHEAD PROJECTORS

Both the opaque and overhead projectors are valuable means of noting specific points, motivating group discussions, and explaining material through visual demonstrations. Both devices are easy to operate and relatively inexpensive to purchase; however, they are somewhat cumbersome and are often difficult to store in a small area.

An enormous amount of free and inexpensive material is available for use with the opaque projector. Any picture, drawing, magazine illustration, textbook page, or photograph can be used with this simple device. Although the opaque projector is bulky in appearance, it is relatively easy to operate. It is necessary only to (1) insert the material on the metal tray or *platen*, (2) push the tray in place with the lever, and (3) adjust the lens to bring the images into sharp focus.

Opaque projectors can be used to enlarge small pictures for large-scale use on chalkboards, butcher paper, or construction paper. Thus, a small map in the daily newspaper or a drawing from a magazine can be made large enough for all the children in the classroom to see at one time. Therefore, individual study materials may become group study materials.

The opaque projector does not of itself make the aide an effective teacher. There is routine work to be done by the aide, planning to the accomplished, and understanding to be displayed. An important point to remember is that the materials to be projected must be selected with specific purposes in mind. They must be arranged and treated so that they promote learning. With proper use of these materials, a good teacher aide can soon become a better teacher aide.

The overhead projector is a valuable device for projecting transparencies on a screen, wall, or chalkboard. One of its special advantages is that it does not even require a screen, and the room does not need to be darkened while the students are viewing the transparencies. The teacher or aide sits or stands facing the class while using this projector. Although overhead transparencies may be already prepared, most teachers prefer to do their own. The transparencies may either be prepared prior to the class session or be made spontaneously during a class discussion. The transparencies may also be erased or enlarged in order to stress a particular point.

Aide-constructed transparencies are usually made by using either a grease pencil or a felt-tip pen to draw the illustrations on a sheet of plastic. To prevent smudging, you should always start drawing or writing in the center of the transparency and work toward the edges. After the transparency is placed on the glass top of the projector, the image is then reflected upward to a mirror attached to a rod above the box. The resulting image is reflected on the screen or wall behind the operator.

Obviously, the advantages in using the overhead projector are many. An instructor facing the class at all times can easily observe class reactions to the presentation and make needed changes or adjustments. Unspoken questions can be observed on students' faces by an alert instructor. Using the projector in a lighted room makes it possible for other types of instruction to be conducted at the same time.

Suggestions for Utilizing Opaque and Overhead Projectors

1. Preview the material or prepare it before the class begins.
2. Arrange the material in the proper sequence for showing.
3. Follow the manufacturer's directions for operating the projector.
4. Leave the image on the screen long enough to permit students to study it.

5. Reshow material as it becomes necessary.
6. Encourage students to prepare their own illustrations and transparencies.
7. Stand beside the teaching aid and not in front of it.
8. Always classify and file your teaching materials.

RECORDS AND TAPES

Records and tapes are invaluable yet relatively inexpensive tools for learning. Both records and tapes are effective ways of arousing student interest, and both can be used for review, practice, and even testing. In addition, both machines can be stopped for questions or discussion, thus allowing maximum student participation. While there is a great variety of educational tapes available, the teacher or teacher aide can easily make her own tapes to meet specific instructional objectives. Furthermore, tapes are extremely flexible — they can be edited, erased, spliced, and used repeatedly.

Educational records are available on every conceivable subject. Perhaps you or a student may have a personal collection of records, some of which may be appropriate for the lesson being presented. Records can be used in a variety of different ways. In music class, students can enjoy listening to a violin solo; in reading, they can listen to the telling of a children's classic. Records can also be used in conjunction with other multimedia aids. For example, in a music class, the words of a song can be shown by using the overhead projector while students sing along with the music on the tape or record. Filmstrips accompanied by correlated tapes or records are readily available in most media centers or libraries. At all instructional levels, records and tapes are an excellent tool for helping youngsters learn to listen more efficiently. Listening to tapes is a valuable activity for purposes of providing feedback and self-evaluation. Tapes can be played back immediately after being recorded, thereby providing quick information and evaluation. In addition, tapes can be played repeatedly with little loss of fidelity, clearness, or volume. Many classrooms use tapes as part of their ongoing program for individualized instruction. Other teachers use tapes to provide a quick review for students who have been absent from class due to illness.

The following suggestions outline some important steps to follow in using tapes in the classroom:

1. Always try to record in a room with as good acoustics as possible.
2. Place the tape recorder on a firm, level surface.
3. Limit outside interruptions, if possible.
4. If students are using the recorder, ask them to speak in a clear, distinct voice.
5. Store tapes in a cabinet where the temperature is between 60°F and 70°F.
6. Index large collections of tapes by title, subject, and number.

CONSTRUCTING BULLETIN BOARDS

At one time, the bulletin board was thought of as a place used primarily for posting notices or pinning up clippings, pictures, cartoons, or other items of assorted interest. Little attention was given to correlating the display with the instructional program of the classroom. The modern concept of using the bulletin board is that it has an instructional function to perform. Bulletin boards can be used for a variety of purposes — to introduce units, to display work, to note holidays and special events, and to emphasize current events.

Visitors to a classroom can often tell a great deal about the school by looking at its bulletin boards. Bulletin boards reveal something about the philosophy of learning that prevails in the class, the use the teacher makes of varied instructional materials, and the nature of the classroom curriculum. Colorful and sprightly bulletin boards indicate a strong desire to stimulate learning while dull, dusty, seldom-changed displays often indicate an indifferent attitude on the part of the teacher and the aide.

From kindergarten through high school, it is possible for the bulletin board to be a focal point for basic learning. In the primary grades, bulletin boards are especially useful for developing students' interests and skills in language arts. In the intermediate grades, imaginative displays can teach the basic knowledge and research required in science and other subjects. In secondary schools, the bulletin board may inspire creative work in art and action research in social studies. While many of the values of bulletin boards are obvious, some are not so apparent. The following are but a few of the benefits to be gained from well-planned bulletin boards:

- Provide for common social experiences through group work in arranging displays
- Furnish an outlet for the artistic and creative abilities of students
- Unify class spirit by creating a feeling of belonging and responsibility
- Energize work in the instructional program when properly coordinated with the curriculum

Planning and setting up interesting and satisfying bulletin boards is a relatively easy task. The following are suggested steps for setting up a bulletin board or display:

Step 1 — Decide on the learning concept or principle you wish the students to learn. The emphasis should be on a single idea or theme. An example is "Good Health Practices."

Step 2 — Begin construction by selecting captions. Captivating captions or titles will attract attention. Posing startling questions or pointed statements are also good attention getters. Example: "My Language is Showing!" or "What I Always Wanted to Know About Science But Was Afraid to Ask!"

Step 3 — Illustrate the theme selected for the bulletin board by gathering a wide variety of pictures, cartoons, etc., and by having students construct their own materials. Remember that the materials are attached to the bulletin board.

Step 4 — Artistic arrangement is essential to an effective display. Keep it uncluttered. The vacant spaces on the bulletin board should just about equal the picture area in order to produce a pleasing balance. Color makes the display bold and forceful. It might be well to have one color for the background and one or two coordinated colors for the captions.

Step 5 — Lettering ties the display together. Labels must be crisp, clear, and accurate. Simplicity in letter design is usually more effective than fancy lettering.

Step 6 — After the above five steps are completed, the task is almost finished. The posting of the display should be done by the students under the supervision of a teacher or aide.

Step 7 — After the bulletin board has served its purpose, it may be taken down and stored in a folder or large envelope for possible modification and use again next year.

DO'S AND DON'TS FOR BULLETIN BOARDS

DO

DO capitalize on all bulletin board space in the classroom.

DO use bulletin boards to arouse student interest.

DO use bulletin boards to follow through on other teaching aids.

DO use pertinent illustrations.

DO arrange materials in an orderly and interesting manner.

DO create original titles.

DO use color harmony and balance.

DO make bulletin boards tell a story.

DO place captions on all illustrations.

DO place bulletin boards where they can be easily seen by all students.

DO collect suitable materials for bulletin boards.

DON'T

DON'T use only commercially prepared materials.

DON'T have more than one theme per display.

DON'T clutter up the bulletin board with too many illustrations.

DON'T keep the same bulletin board for too long a period of time.

DON'T construct a bulletin board and then ignore it for instructional purposes.

Good educational practices require that bulletin boards be more than simple artwork. This is not to say that bulletin boards should not be neat and appealing, but most of all, they should be meaningful to the students. All classroom activities should be reevaluated to ensure maximum student participation. Students should share in lesson planning and development and feel true involvement in the teaching-learning process.

MATERIALS PREPARATION

With relatively little advanced training and with simple directions from the teacher or media specialist, aides can prepare such multimedia items as overhead transparencies, tapes, models, charts, and picture files. This preparation of "software" is vital to the development of an effective classroom multimedia program.

The commercial enterprises that sell the audiovisual equipment used in most schools are important sources of training for aides in the preparation of media materials. Many of these companies offer evening and Saturday workshops for both the professional staff and teacher aides. Usually this service is free, and most of the training is of excellent quality. Other important sources of training in material preparation are curriculum centers at nearby universities and colleges. Many educational departments in institutions of higher learning now include courses on preparation and use of media materials in their basic curriculum. More than likely, you would be welcome to take these courses. In addition, if your school district has a media specialist, he or she could be another important source of training in this field.

To the greatest extent possible, aides should be utilized in preparing audiovisual materials. For instance, one inexpensive, easy-to-use, and highly successful aid is the write-on slide. This film is a specially treated clear slide that is coated so that it can be drawn or written on and can be projected with a regular slide projector. Although the best images are obtained with drawing ink made especially for use on drafting film, images can be formed by using almost any pencil or felt-tip pen. Transfer letters may also be used.

Write-on slides can be used by teachers and aides for review questions, to show diagrams, and as flash cards. Other teachers have used slides to illustrate oral reports; as drill and skill activities for early readiness training; as phonics review slides for independent study; as follow-up activities after field trips; and as individual expression around a specific theme. Creative teachers and aides should be able to find many other uses for such a flexible, yet inexpensive, teaching aid.

Other materials you might consider constructing include science charts and folders explaining experiments, word charts, and listening tapes. Pretaped stories and lessons filed in a listening center can be of great assistance to slow learners. Tapes have many additional advantages. They can be used for small group or individual drill, for students who are ill and miss practice in basic processes, and for those who need special help.

PRINTED TEACHING AIDS

Most of us are amateurs when it comes to displaying artistic talents, but anyone who can write or type can effectively prepare duplicated materials. In addition to good textbooks, there is a frequent need for special printed or duplicated teaching aids. These aids, usually referred to as *handouts* or *worksheets*, are prepared to meet a specific instructional objective.

The actual preparation depends on the method to be used and the type of equipment available. Once you master a few basic points, making duplicated or mimeographed teaching aids is easy. After you and the teacher have decided on the method to be used, follow the simple, easy-to-follow instructions provided below:

1. The material should be simple, concise, and clear.
2. The material should be illustrated as fully as the need requires. Pictures and drawing often illustrate a point much more vividly than words.
3. The material prepared should be appealing to the students so that it encourages them to read and study the material.
4. The material should be of a size that is convenient for use.

Preparing well-organized and clear duplication and mimeograph stencils is an important function of the teacher aide. The following basic steps in mimeograph stencil preparation should help you provide better service to students and teachers:

I. Planning position on the stencil
   A. Place guide sheet between stencil sheet and backing.
   B. Top edge of paper should come to the line designating the top line guide for impression paper.
   C. Holding these sheets up to the light, make sure that the work falls within the limitation lines.
II. Typing the stencil
   A. The typewriter
      1. Shift ribbon out of printing position.
      2. Brush type thoroughly to remove ribbon ink.
   B. The stencil
      1. Insert cushion sheet between stencil sheeting and backing.
      2. Place smooth side out on all three copies.
   C. Insert stencil into typewriter
      1. Insert all three sheets with the backing next to the platen.
      2. Align stencil so number markings on both sides of the stencil correspond.
   D. Typing
      1. Type slowly.
      2. Use uniform touch.
      3. Check periodically to make sure stencil is not wrinkling.
III. Correcting errors
   A. Correction fluid
      1. Apply a coating of correction fluid over the mistake, allow to dry, then retype over letter or letters to be corrected.

ADDITIONAL MULTIMEDIA DUTIES

Only through proper training and systematic planning is it possible to make effective use of multimedia aids and equipment. The experiences that teacher aides gain can be most worthwhile, but it is essential that they be given effective supervision in planning media usage and that they be assigned tasks that contribute to the education of children in the classroom. Routine media tasks soon lose their challenge if variety is not provided in daily assignments.

The following list of multimedia tasks for teacher aides should contribute to an effective audiovisual program in your classroom:

- Preparing posters, charts, and other visual aids through dry mounting
- Laminating visual teaching aids
- Checking out and returning films, tapes, etc.
- Making transparencies for the overhead projector
- Working with photography equipment and developing film
- Preparing Spirit® masters and stencil masters
- Setting up and operating tape recorders, filmstrip projectors, opaque projectors, etc.
- Writing to companies and organizations for free media materials
- Preparing classroom bulletin boards and displays
- Collecting pictures and other materials for class work
- Keeping an inventory of all media equipment in the building
- Providing information to aid teachers in the selection of new media software
- Giving assistance to students who are working on media projects
- Supervising live videotaping in the classroom
- Keeping media equipment in good condition (cleaning, changing lamps, etc.)
- Doing Thermo-Fax® copying when requested

SUMMARY

Modern educators realize that since a child cannot get every experience firsthand, learning through multimedia materials is the next best method available. Through various media, children may have experiences that, while indirect, approximate reality. Experiences with audiovisual materials can help children understand phenomena not in their immediate environment — how they look and sound, how they operate, what their uses are.

As a teacher aide works with children, in groups and individually, her work is made effective if she makes full use of learning resources available to her. In addition to the textbook, these resources include films, filmstrips, tape recorders, overhead projectors, and record players. The teacher aide needs to become familiar with the operation of the major kinds of audiovisual equipment, as well as with the procedures to be followed for scheduling their use in the school where she works. By following the specific recommendations that have been made for effective utilization of major types of multimedia equipment and materials, the aide should greatly increase her effectiveness in the classroom.

CHAPTER 9

WORKING IN SPECIAL AREAS

UP to this point, emphasis has been placed on the role of the teacher aide in the regular classroom. Yet most schools find that aides can be of service to children in many additional areas beyond the regular classroom. For instance, an aide can lend valuable assistance to the teaching staff on the school playground since it is likely that she is younger than the average teacher and is thus able to participate more energetically in the children's playtime activities. If the aide has a background in athletics or physical education, she can easily make play periods more productive and meaningful for the youngsters.

Likewise, some schools find that aides are useful for releasing teachers from supervisory tasks, such as hall or cafeteria duty. By releasing teachers and other school personnel from tedious, routine chores, aides free the teaching staff to concentrate their efforts on more specialized instructional functions. Other schools utilize teacher aides as support personnel in special education classes, while still other schools elect to employ aides as library assistants or as aides to the counselor.

Whatever specialized task you perform, you need specific training and detailed instructions in order to handle it well. Too often, aides assume that if a task does not require instructional expertise, they can accomplish it without formal preparation or specific directions. However, most educators agree that an aide should not be assigned supervisory or administrative duties by herself outside the regular classroom until she demonstrates her competence and proficiency in handling typical situations that are likely to arise. If an aide assigned to the playground or cafeteria does not feel secure in her ability to handle the assignment, serious problems can and will develop.

Unfortunately, many aides feel that duties outside the regular classroom are unpleasant and unimportant. Nothing could be

155

further from the truth. Areas such as playgrounds, school cafeterias, and libraries contain some of the most vital and productive areas of the school, because it is here that children carry on much of their social life and learn how to get along with others. These auxiliary areas outside the regular classroom are integral parts of every school; certainly, significant learning takes place here as well as in the classroom.

ASSISTING ON THE PLAYGOUND

A primary concern of today's elementary schools is that of improving the physical fitness of growing children through participation in playground activities. These activities provide youngsters with opportunities to release their pent-up emotional and physical energies and to discover and develop desirable social habits. Here they experience and internalize important developmental concepts, such as fast, slow, up, down, over, under, and through. Also, playground activities help children learn to communicate as they express their ideas and feelings through physical movement and verbal exchange. As children acquire essential skills and expanded understandings that enhance their self-confidence, they learn the value of both competition and cooperation.

The relatively unstructured play periods before school, during recess, and through the noon lunch period provide teachers as well as aides with numerous opportunities to observe children in a natural environment. Through observation of playground activities, you learn to distinguish the leaders from the followers, the cheerful from the melancholy, the friendly from the hostile, and the shy from the boisterous. Likewise, playground supervision presents you with opportunities to develop friendships with children outside the regular classroom environment. Casual friendships developed on the playground often help youngsters to see you in an entirely different light. Positive playground experiences encourage children to respect and admire the teacher aide as a person. Building favorable rapport with the children on the playground potentially can make your job more pleasant as well as motivate the students to be more cooperative with you in the classroom.

As a playground supervisor, you can be sure of one thing: You will never become bored or wonder what to do next. At various times, you will need to mediate an argument, stop a fight, repair a bruised ego, or negotiate a settlement regarding the use of playground equipment. At other times your attention is called to handling such emergencies as a skinned knee, a blackened eye, or even a broken arm. However, you can provide your greatest help to children when you suggest games, teach playground activities, and interact with the children, all the while demonstrating sportsmanship conduct and attitudes for them to emulate. By teaching children the standard playground games and by demonstrating activities that teach the proper use of playground equipment, you can provide a great deal of fun while developing the children's physical and social skills as well.

Playground supervision is exciting and rewarding, but you should remember that legal consequences are likely to follow negligent supervision. It is the duty of the school and its supervising personnel to make certain that play areas are safe and free from hazardous conditions. An aide assigned to supervise a playground is not expected to be in all places at all times; however, she must be reasonably prudent and should circulate among the students so that she can readily determine when hazardous activities develop or are being pursued. It is the school administrator's duty to keep teacher aides posted of any safety hazards present on the playground.

Even one school accident is one too many. Constant vigilance by teachers and aides pays high dividends when it comes to the health and safety of school children. Be alert to safety hazards that may be caused by the weather. For example, rain produces slippery entrances; wind turns doors into dangerous, moving objects; ice creates obvious possibilities for slipping and falling. Even certain times of the school day create special hazards in and of themselves and greatly increase the potential for injury to youngsters. When students run for a bus after school or when eager children push to be first in line as they reenter the school building after recess, they can easily bring about safety hazards for themselves as well as others.

Inexperienced teachers and aides often overlook dangers posed by vehicular traffic on adjacent streets. One careless error in judgment might easily cost a youngster his life or leave him crippled. Make a constant, conscious effort to station yourself between children at play and the nearby streets. Youngsters should be continually warned and reminded of the dangers present when their play takes them close to traffic.

When you are in direct authority over children on the playground, it is just as important to follow proper procedures when unacceptable behavior occurs as it is when you are in the classroom. Even on a well-supervised playground, instances of unacceptable behavior occur, but many behavior problems can be prevented. For example, most fights can be avoided if an alert teacher or aide anticipates trouble and takes corrective measures. Excessively rough play often causes sensitive egos to be bruised or tempers to flare, with the predictable result of a shouting match which can quickly develop into a physical confrontation. Hostile looks accompanied by threatening stances and gestures are danger signs indicating that volatile behavior is likely to ensue unless someone in authority steps over to "break it up." Give your immediate attention to these types of situations and thereby forestall needless, counterproductive altercations from developing on the playground. Once you successfully prevent playground misunderstandings from running their inevitable, destructive course, then follow up your first action with the diversionary technique of focusing the problem child's attention upon other interests. For best results, see to it that troublesome children go to opposite sides of the playground where they have limited possibilities for scheduling a rematch.

The following hints will prove helpful to you in preventing playground disturbances:

1. Always be punctual for your duty assignment.
2. Be constantly alert while on duty.
3. Know your area of responsibility on the playground.
4. Make sure you are highly visible to students at all times.
5. Don't join in games with children on a regular basis,

since this practice limits your field of supervision.

6. Don't let adults monopolize your time through excessive socializing.
7. Know exactly what to do in emergency situations.
8. If a potential trouble spot is observed, go to it immediately in a calm manner. Above all, don't get bystanders excited by showing your alarm.
9. When a dispute takes place, isolate those involved and listen quietly to both sides of the story.
10. If the dispute appears to be getting out of control or if a dangerous situation develops, send for assistance immediately.

CAFETERIA DUTY

Learning does not stop when the school bell rings to dismiss the class for lunch. Time spent in the school cafeteria provides unlimited opportunities for valuable lessons in social, cultural, and nutritional areas. It is a reality of life, however, that supervision of some sort must be provided in the cafeteria during the lunch period. Often, teachers and aides are scheduled on a rotating basis to supervise the cafeteria, with particular attention given to the serving line.

Cafeteria supervision is often a troublesome, thankless task, for without a doubt, the lunch period is one of the most difficult times to try to contain normal, energetic children for any length of time. When children approach the cafeteria, they are usually hungry, full of youthful energy, and eager to socialize with their friends. Once in the cafeteria, they tend to be careless about carrying their food to the table and tend not to see persons and objects who stand between them and their objective. The end result is a trail of litter and debris consisting of straw papers, milk cartons, runaway silverware, and any food items that are not firmly attached to the tray. Accidents do happen. You are probably in the wrong assignment if you are upset by overturned orange juice, sloshed soup, or an occasional child who, innocently enough, collides with you head-on because he was busily swapping his hamburger for his friend's dessert on the way to the lunch table. When the unforeseen occurs, try not to panic; rather, send for the custodian, who probably has already been apprised of the disaster and is on his way to repair the damage.

Obviously, some basic ground rules must be established if the cafeteria is to be properly supervised by teachers and aides. In order to achieve success as a cafeteria aide, you should attempt to get meaningful, well-defined answers to the following questions from teachers and/or administrators:

1. How many teacher aides are assigned to cafeteria duty and what specific area will each cover?
2. How much authority will you have over students in the cafeteria? Will you be permitted to send recalcitrant students to the office or to change their seating arrangement?
3. What procedures should you follow if a child becomes ill or injured?
4. Is it permissible for children to leave the cafeteria to go to the lavatory or to their lockers?
5. What should you do if one or more students become unruly?
6. What kind of atmosphere does the school administration want the cafeteria to reflect?

Too often, teacher aides assigned to cafeteria duty forget that teaching proper social behavior can be a long, seemingly interminable, process that requires much patience on their part. Inevitably, youngsters forget or ignore school rules and act as if they never heard of table manners. It would be well to remember that a simple request to cease and desist from unacceptable behavior can take a variety of forms. Requests intended to effect a change in behavior can take such wordless forms as giving the child a meaningful glance, walking slowly but purposefully in the child's direction, or simply touching his shoulder. Regrettably, when students do not respond to simple requests to behave, aides frequently fall into the foolhardy trap of raising their voices and scolding the child. Such emotional outbursts seldom accomplish their intended purpose. Aides who scold loudly and threaten students are usually ineffective and not respected. Their loud warnings give pause the first time or two that the children hear them, but thereafter their words become progressively more ineffective as the scolding is repeated over and over again. What is worse, an aide who resorts to yelling or threatening often becomes the favorite subject of a juvenile Rich Little impersonator who, when the aide's back is turned, entertains all those within earshot with uproarious renditions — complete with exaggerated facial expressions — of the aide's latest parry with the young rebels.

Once on the job in the cafeteria you will find the following hints helpful:

1. Keep cool. Losing your temper does little to help a problem situation.
2. Don't ignore misbehavior; correct it calmly and quietly as soon as possible.
3. Don't let personal emotions regarding the child interfere with your good judgment when taking disciplinary action.
4. If a dangerous situation develops, send for help immediately.
5. Think positive thoughts.

SERVING IN THE LIBRARY

The need for good library services in a modern school is a well-accepted fact. Schools that realize their obligation to the students and provide superior library facilities and services for their students are usually rewarded with superior educational programs. In a sense, the nature and scope of library services serve as a partial index and provide clues to the outside observer regarding the character and quality of curriculum and instruction within the school.

School libraries are expected to fulfill certain basic educational functions. They facilitate the instruction of students and aid them in developing research techniques. They help youngsters to learn correct study habits, proper attitudes, and to behave with consideration for their fellow students when they are working in the library. As an aide, you should endeavor to stimulate their interest in independent investigation; encourage them to read for enjoyment and pleasure. Moreover, as you observe the students' independent and voluntary use of the school library, you will receive fresh and valuable new insights into students' behavior, interests, and individual potentialities.

Library aides perform a variety of nonprofessional tasks under the direction of a certificated librarian or other supervisor. Keeping library cards and records in order, assisting students in locating reference materials, mending and repairing torn books and magazines, and keeping the library shelves neat and orderly are some of the important functions you will have. In an understaffed library, a teacher aide is a priceless asset.

Everyone agrees that youngsters who want to become proficient in the use of library resources must master certain basic skills. Included in these basic skills are learning the arrangement and classification of materials; gaining knowledge of the card catalog as well as the various approaches to its use; acquiring an understanding of dictionaries, indexes, and other specialized reference tools; and developing an appreciation of books and other resources. In attempting to reach these goals, the library aide assists children in mastering the following kinds of special skills by learning:

1. Proper use of materials
2. Circulation policies and procedures
3. Card catalog usage
4. Special reference book usage
5. How to make and use bibliographies

No matter what their size, schools will improve the efficiency of their library services when the following duties are performed by teacher aides:

- Assisting students in selecting books and other materials
- Typing catalog cards, book cards, orders, and reports
- Assisting the librarian in taking inventory
- Checking out books and equipment to students and teachers
- Keeping the librarian informed of needed supplies
- Providing teachers with lists of students with overdue books

- Writing to companies and organizations for free materials
- Reviewing monthly magazines and bulletins for items of interest to staff members
- Reading stories to small groups of students
- Stimulating students' interest in new topics by setting up interest centers
- Circulating lists of new materials to teachers
- Reshelving books in their proper places so they can be located quickly and easily
- Keeping the appearance of the library in good order

WORKING IN THE SCHOOL OFFICE

The school office, the hub of school activity, is certainly an area that makes one of the greatest contributions to the efficiency and effectiveness of the ongoing school program. Often a teacher aide works in the office to assist the school secretary with her wide variety of office duties. An aide assigned to the school office soon discovers that she has little time for socializing or idle chatter.

An effective office aide possesses such important attributes as above-average intelligence, a pleasing personality, honesty, loyalty, good judgment, emotional stability, and the ability to take care of emergencies. She has sufficient clerical skill to type accurately forty words per minute. While shorthand is desirable, it is not usually a requirement; however, she should be able to compose routine letters and bulletins, spell correctly, and use proper punctuation and grammar. An ability to understand filing procedures is essential. Equally important is the ability to know when to handle a problem herself and when to refer the problem to the secretary or principal. She has a good self-image, and her actions show that she gets along well with other office workers. Great emphasis is also placed on her ability to meet the public and to project a positive image for the school.

Aides assigned to the school office are usually given such tasks as answering the telephone, taking care of ill or injured children, calling mothers to bring forgotten lunch money, handling lost-and-found items, and mollifying irate parents until the principal arrives. Aides also assist teachers with questions and problems falling within their jurisdiction, but under no circumstances do aides handle disciplinary cases sent to the office. If the principal is not present to handle the matter, the aide either calls upon a designated teacher or delays the disciplinary action until the principal returns. In addition, office aides receive office phone calls and visitors, screen their requests, route them to the appropriate persons, make appointments, and furnish information.

A large part of the office aide's work involves relationships with fellow workers. The atmosphere created in the school office depends greatly upon the secretary and office aide. In order to get along with fellow workers, the aide should try to develop a friendly atmosphere within the school office. Your ability to get along with school personnel is greatly enhanced if you are a friendly person. For example, at appropriate moments you might want to compliment a teacher on her new hair style or a becoming dress; congratulate the members of the winning faculty bowling team; or praise the custodian for the neat appearance of the school cafeteria.

Working with students, parents, and the general public involves the office aide in establishing and maintaining good public relations for the school, its teachers, and the principal. In order to perform these duties well, you must be a true public servant and have other people's interests at heart. You must learn to accept interruptions even while you are concentrating on the details of your own work. Your performance reveals your personality — it will make friends or foes for the school.

COUNSELOR AIDE

The school counselor is a member of the regular school staff who shares many of the responsibilities of other staff members. The counselor's training, knowledge, skills, and experience make him a valuable resource person for both teachers and students. His talents contribute to the personal and social development of all children within the school, thus enhancing the emotional development and education of children by promoting better self-understanding, by encouraging the use of special services, and by locating and referring children and parents to other services outside the school, whenever appropriate.

An aide assigned to the school counselor will probably find herself doing some initial interviewing of students, helping children to complete forms, and arranging for appointments with the counselor. Even more importantly, she makes home visits to provide the counselor with information about youngster's home environment. Aides who live in the community served by the school can be extremely helpful in this capacity since the parents and children served by the school are likely to be more relaxed with the aide than they would be with the counselor.

Further, aides who are residents of the community, particularly in lower socioeconomic and minority cultures, probably can communicate more effectively with parents than can other school personnel who are new to the community. In this same context, aides familiar with community attitudes and who are "on top of" problem situations may be able to "rap" with children regarding the school situation, thereby preventing problems from arising in the first place. By giving visitors to the counselor's office an understanding and friendly reception, an encouraging word, and a sympathetic smile, the counselor's aide serves to put anxious students and nervous parents at ease.

The following suggested duties for counselor aides are of a general nature and should prove useful as a guide in working with the school counselor:

1. Assist in administering standardized tests
2. Aid in compiling case studies
3. Help with group guidance activities
4. Assist with orientation programs
5. Assist with parent contacts
6. Help in disseminating social, educational, and vocational information
7. Aid in locating students who need specialized services
8. Assist in observing and recording student behavior

ASSISTING THE NURSE

All health services provided by the school center around one key person, the school nurse. The school nurse should have training and experience not only in health, first aid, and nursing, but she should also enjoy working with children and be able to relate well with them at their various levels of interest and understanding. It is her duty to serve as an advisor regarding school safety and to help develop safety consciousness in children. In addition, the nurse should be willing to assist teachers in developing health education programs in their classrooms, investigate home conditions, and keep vital health records up-to-date.

A school nurse often loses valuable time in the simple routine of communicating with other staff members within the building. She would be better served by having written memos placed in teachers' mailboxes than by carrying on lengthy conversations with individual teachers. At such times, an aide can be a handy time-saver to the busy nurse. Likewise, an aide can help the nurse by typing letters, distributing health materials, duplicating essential health forms, making appointments for children at clinics or doctor's offices, setting up health workshops, and arranging for various medical tests.

An aide assigned to the school nurse provides numerous services to both the professional staff and to the children attending the school. Such an aide helps with inoculations, gives initial vision and hearing examinations, and learns to keep accurate health records. If the professional nurse is required to serve several different schools, the nurse's aide can keep the nurse informed as to which students require immediate attention or special care during her next scheduled visit to that particular school.

Several first aid kits containing emergency supplies should always be kept on hand to be loaned out for use on the playground, field trips, and after-school activities. Many schools have the nurse's aide make up first aid kits and distribute them to each classroom so that teachers can take care of minor problems. When this is done, the aide can further assist the nurse by giving teachers instructions regarding first aid procedures.

In addition, nurse's aides provide such services as administering first aid treatment for minor cuts or bruises, taking ill children home, or staying in the sick room with ill or injured children whose parents cannot be reached. Many schools use nurse's aides to help weigh and measure students once or twice a year, check posture from time to time, and make room inspections periodically, especially during times when there are epidemics of flu, measles, chicken pox, or the common cold.

However, it must be stressed that at no time does the aide replace the nurse in her professional service to children. She has neither the training nor the experience to decide how seriously ill or hurt a child may be. The aide's role is always that of freeing the nurse so she can perform more efficiently and effectively her professional duties with the staff and children.

SPECIAL SUPPORT STAFF

Most schools now have special teachers or consultants such as speech therapists, remedial reading teachers, school social workers, and resource teachers. Even though many schools do not have an adequate number of these special supportive personnel, proper utilization of teacher aides can greatly increase the benefits derived from even a small number of specialists.

Unfortunately, the remedial reading teacher frequently must divide her time between two or more schools. Even if she is assigned to only one school, she often lacks the time to meet daily with each remedial student. Such stressful situations may be alleviated, however, when the remedial reading teacher is assigned an aide, for then she is able to plan individualized instruction in special, prescribed, daily activities for each child. Aides who find themselves in this type of situation must be careful to observe closely the teacher's plans when carrying out activities prepared by the reading specialist.

Aides assigned to special education classrooms will find themselves performing tasks on a one-to-one basis with the children as they work on skills of a basic nature. It must be stressed that aides who are assigned to work with trainable mentally handicapped and educable mentally handicapped classes require some special personality characteristics beyond the general qualities previously discussed in this book. Teacher aides in special education classrooms need to be mature individuals. Bizarre behavior, such as unusual or irrational actions and noises, are often displayed and must not disturb her or throw her off balance. She needs a strong stomach to survive the occasional unpleasant smells and sights. She needs a special type of compassion — one that recognizes and seeks to fulfill the needs of the special education child.

Today, increasing numbers of school systems throughout the United States are providing facilities within their schools for physically handicapped children. In spite of their physical handicaps, these youngsters usually are emotionally, socially, and intellectually ready to participate in regular classroom work. In some cases, they spend part of each school day in special classrooms where they work at therapy activities and then spend the remainder of the day in the regular classroom. Aides assigned to this kind of special program perform many tasks oriented to physical therapy and to helping the handicapped child get around in the school building. She may also have tasks geared to keeping records of the children's progress in physical therapy sessions.

Aides who work in specialized roles need special courses or workshop experiences in order to be of the greatest service to specialized teachers and to meet the complex needs of the children. All children are alike in that they all need encouragement, understanding, motivation, and an environment conducive to learning. However, children with physical or mental handicaps need a special environment that provides certain types of equipment and materials geared to their special learning needs and abilities.

SUMMARY

This chapter has attempted to make clear the fact that teacher aides can be of service to children in many areas outside the regular classroom. Even though the aide has little formal training, she can help make a good teacher still more effective. Often merely adding another pair of eyes and ears makes it possible to gain insight into certain situations that, alone, even the best teacher would have missed. Aides' nonprofessional backgrounds sometimes bestow subtle understandings that teachers who have been "programmed" in their thinking and experience could never have uncovered. Occasionally their "amateurism" proves to be smarter, more appropriate, and to contain more common sense than the trained, professional, predictable approaches of the teaching staff.

Assuredly, children benefit directly from an aide's participation in activities beyond the regular classroom. Such activities often result in richer, more personal, and more varied experiences for the children. But children benefit indirectly, also, since aides tend to keep teachers fresher and more alive. Aides help save them from some degree of weariness and discouragement that sets in from doing the seemingly endless chores that are a part of teaching: housekeeping tasks, clerical chores, administrative tasks, and the many routine instructional tasks that go on behind the scene before the children ever arrive at school. Aides who share the teaching work load provide an invaluable service — that of letting the teacher give more of herself to her children.

CHAPTER 10

EVALUATING YOURSELF

THE purpose of evaluating an aide's performance — assessing skills, techniques, and methods — is to generate improvement. Evaluation is not an end in itself, but rather a means of discovering what changes are needed and for determining the direction in which the changes are to be made. Evaluation, in its broadest sense, is a continuous process of gathering information so that job performance can be monitored and studied to determine the effectiveness of the person's performance.

Most educators agree that the most effective method of evaluation is self-evaluation. However, self-evaluation requires a high degree of maturity, as well as a great deal of introspection on the part of the teacher aide. It requires that the individual hold a mirror up to herself and then proceed to look objectively at her actual situation, not just see what she desires to find. Underlying effective self-evaluation are an attitude of openness and a trust in others. These requirements demand a strong self-concept that can handle constructive self-criticism and, at the same time, be tolerant of other workers' faults and mistakes.

If you want to grow and improve your service to teachers and children, you must desire to change. You must develop your own standards of satisfactory and superior performance. It requires a special quality of insight to judge how closely your expectations of yourself measure up to your actual performance. Unless you recognize your own strengths and weaknesses, the evaluation process will have little permanent influence on your classroom performance and effectiveness.

Finally, most teacher aides are evaluated from the standpoint of how effectively and efficiently they carry out their assignments, their interpersonal relationships with other staff members, their general attitudes, and how well they comply with their school's rules and regulations. Although most school

170

systems use some form of teacher and/or administrator evaluation, supplementing this external evaluation with self-evaluation can bring about changes that significantly benefit the teacher aide's performance.

IMPROVING YOUR EFFECTIVENESS

How do you know if your performance as a teacher aide is satisfactory? It is doubtful that a paper-and-pencil examination would be the most effective way to measure aide efficiency. A better method, of course, is to review all the roles the teacher aide must fill and measure yourself against role expectations to see how effectively you are performing these duties. If it were possible for you to secure a list of responsibilities that fit your job description, you and your supervisor could review the job description together, discussing each item on the list as your supervisor spelled out his or her expectations of you. Practical considerations make it necessary for you and your supervisor to agree on job expectations and to perceive them in the same light.

As an alternative to having a conference with your supervisor, you might choose to ask yourself the following kinds of questions:

1. Do I effectively help the classroom teacher to assist more students by giving her more time for individualized instruction?
2. Have I made the classroom teacher aware of various talents and interests I possess that might be useful resources for the class?
3. Am I able to identify and assist children who are experiencing learning problems?
4. Do I contribute to the classroom by continuously evaluating my role and making suggestions regarding additional assignments?
5. Do I show resourcefulness in helping to provide enrichment experiences for students?
6. Do I assume an active role in planning instructional objectives and activities with the classroom teacher?

7. Am I acquainted with and do I follow school rules and policies?
8. Do I respect the rights, feelings, and opinions of others?
9. Do I show evidence of constructive professional growth?
10. Do I avoid criticizing children, teachers, administrators, or the school?
11. Do I willingly accept constructive criticism as a means of increasing my personal and professional growth?
12. Do I observe the classroom teacher's successful teaching techniques so that I might continue to learn?

AIDE RESPONSIBILITIES

As already stated, an effective teacher-teacher aide relationship is fundamental to achieving a basic understanding of the aide's responsibilities and the teacher's expectations. The objectives and responsibilities of an aide working in a school setting should be clearly defined before she ever signs her employment contract. An aide should never be left to wonder, "What should I be doing now?"

Most teachers and aides find that an open and professional understanding of the aide's role usually helps to avoid feelings of anxiety and an unpleasant relationship. When a misunderstanding occurs, it is always best to face the problem openly and promptly. In this way, a promising, fruitful partnership is less likely to dissolve into disappointment for one or both individuals. More than one teacher aide has worked for months, believing that her work was satisfactory, only to find during the formal evaluation process that all the while her supervisor was dissatisfied with her performance. When substantive issues are brushed aside and not faced squarely, difficulties inevitably crop up.

Although differences of opinion are to be expected in any human endeavor, conflicts between a teacher and her aide are counter-productive and become increasingly destructive to their working relationship as long as they continue. When serious and irreconcilable differences do occur, often the teacher aide must be either transferred or dismissed. However, before such drastic action is taken, every effort should be made to try to resolve the conflict and to reestablish a meaningful relationship. The welfare of the children should be the ultimate determining factor when making the decision to retain a teacher or aide or to dismiss her.

Teacher aides should be given numerous opportunities to continue learning about their jobs. Teachers are never satisfied that they "know all the answers," and it follows that teacher aides should also strive to learn more about their jobs and to get better acquainted with new ideas and procedures in their field. By attending faculty meetings regularly, they can gain a greater understanding and awareness of their school's operation. If the professional staff is engaged in in-service education activities, aides should also be given the opportunity to attend these sessions. General information and resource materials distributed to regular classroom teachers should also be given to aides if the materials relate to the aides' assignments.

Finally, aides should try to find time in their busy schedules to talk with their supervising teachers in terms of "How am I doing?" and "How might I improve?" It is the teacher who bears the greatest responsibility for helping you to improve your skills, but you, too, have a share in that responsibility. An aide who truly wants to be of service welcomes the opportunity to meet with her supervisor and discuss ways she can improve her performance.

CRITERIA FOR EVALUATION

Frequently, the job description for the teacher aide is not clearly stated, and duties are listed only in general terms. For example, a job description might state that the aide is to interact positively with students, but it does not make clear what *interact positively* means or just how she is supposed to accomplish this task. Is she never to criticize the youngsters? One aide may interpret the statement to mean that she is to respect the rights, feelings, and opinions of others. Another aide may feel that it means she is supposed to show interest in and enthusiasm for youngsters. This wide range of possible interpretations of a job description shows us that the first step in an effective evaluation program is to determine what criteria is utilized in appraising one's work.

Likewise, if the primary purpose of the evaluation process is to improve instruction and to upgrade existing teacher aide performances, certainly more emphasis should be placed on student progress than on the aide's personality traits. Presumably a person can be expected to change her work habits and procedures much more easily and readily than she can change her long-established attitudes and basic disposition.

Traditionally, teacher aide evaluations have included the following major categories:

PERSONAL APPEARANCE AND ATTITUDES. Items include attendance, dress, courtesy, temperament, grooming, and willingness to give time and effort to the job.

RELATIONSHIPS WITH CHILDREN. Included are friendliness, fairness, sympathy, helpfulness, liking for children, and skill in resolving conflicts.

RELATIONSHIPS WITH THE CLASSROOM TEACHER. In this category are punctuality, efficient use of time and materials, willingness to accept direction, dependability in meeting commitments and assignments, and initiative and alertness in meeting teacher needs.

SCHOOL-COMMUNITY RELATIONS. This includes demonstrating knowledge of and proper use of channels of communication, using discretion in discussing school and community matters, and showing sufficient awareness and adherance to school policies and routines.

Regardless of what kinds of criteria your school uses to evaluate aides, the criteria should be supportive of the teacher aide rather than punitive. In order for it to do this, the evaluation should be conducted openly, with the aide being kept informed of which aspects of her work are being evaluated, as well as which types of procedures are being utilized to conduct the evaluation. The final results should be shared openly and any differences in perceived expectations should be clarified so that necessary adjustments can be made in teacher aide performance.

UTILIZING SELF-EVALUATION TECHNIQUES

As indicated above, self-evaluation *can* be a highly effective method of teacher aide evaluation. However, it has not been totally accepted by many educators. They believe that many aides, particularly those who are insecure or who lack experience, tend to overrate themselves. They feel that aides who fit this category fool themselves into believing that they are doing as well as could be expected under trying circumstances. Few aides, opponents of self-evaluation point out, are able to be objective and forthright in assessing their own performances; consequently, their self-evaluations are both inaccurate and unreliable.

Nevertheless, educators who adhere to a different philosophy believe that the inadequacies of self-evaluation techniques result not from basic weaknesses in the procedures but, instead, result from the failure of all involved to understand the underlying purposes of teacher aide evaluation; therefore, individuals misuse the technique. In addition, proponents of self-evaluation point out that in an open, nonthreatening relationship between the aide and the supervising teacher, self-evaluation can be a useful motivational tool for self-improvement. If evaluation is regarded, as it should be, as a technique for improving performance rather than as a mere rating system, self-appraisal becomes an important part of the total evaluation process.

Remember, however, that the effectiveness of self-evaluation techniques depends on careful preplanning. First, aides should have an opportunity to have a voice in determining the appropriate items for any checklist or form devised for self-evaluation. Second, teacher aides must be prepared for self-evaluation. The aide must try to see herself objectively, so she can gain accurate insights into her strengths and weaknesses. It is just as important for her to know her strong points as it is for her to be aware of her deficiencies. Finally, when the aide is called upon to evaluate herself, either on a formal evaluation checklist or otherwise, she should be able to understand the relationship her evaluation has to classroom performance. She should never view appraisal as simply a performance rating. Rather, she should see the evaluation process as the opportunity to identify areas where improvement is needed as well as to identify areas where performance is satisfactory.

If a teacher aide is to grow professionally and improve the quality of her services to youngsters, she first must decide to change. In fact, there are some important reasons why self-evaluation can prove useful to a teacher aide. These include the following:

1. Teacher aides usually regard self-evaluation as the most acceptable method for evaluating performance.
2. When self-evaluation techniques are utilized, the aide shares in the responsibility for her own self-improvement.
3. The only effective motive for change is one that is created from within.

Three sample teacher aide self-evaluation forms are provided. However, great benefit is often derived from working cooperatively with administrators, teachers, and other aides to design your own self-evaluation instrument. Such a form, it is hoped, would more nearly meet the needs of your own particular classroom and school.

ACCEPTING CRITICISM

Whether you wish it to be or not, you should be aware that teacher aides are continually being evaluated. Everything you do or say is weighed and measured in some manner, not only by your school's administrators and teachers, but by students, parents, and co-workers as well. Continued evaluation provides opportunities for the proper recognition of areas where you perform successfully and have increasing competence. Recognition for work well done should in turn stimulate you to even greater accomplishments and thus make it easier to maintain a high standard of efficiency. Nevertheless, at times it is necessary for supervisors to correct faults or to discuss inadequacies in

TEACHER AIDE SELF-EVALUATION FORM

Name_____ Date_____

School_____ Assignment_____

Rating Scale: 1 - Acceptable
2 - Needs Improvement
3 - Unsatisfactory

Performance

_____ Cooperate with teacher

_____ Cooperate with students

_____ Complete assignments

_____ Work with accuracy

_____ Show attention to routine matters

_____ Care of equipment and supplies

_____ Demonstrate effective disciplinary techniques

_____ Carry out instructions with minimum of direction

_____ Use materials skillfully

_____ Learn detailed tasks readily

_____ Am thorough

_____ Operate at students' level

Personal Qualities

_____ Am prompt

_____ Show interest in doing a good job

_____ Use acceptable English

_____ Demonstrate responsibility

_____ Show neatness in assigned tasks

_____ Am fair and impartial with students

_____ Accept suggestions for improvement

_____ Have pleasant personal appearance

_____ Have good attendance record

_____ Use discretion in dealing with others

Sample II

HOW DO I RATE AS A TEACHER AIDE?

Name_____ Date_____

School_____ Teacher_____

Key: Indicate A for excellent
B for very good
C for passable
D for poor, needs improvement

_____ 1. Perform routine tasks efficiently

_____ 2. Am willing to put in essential time and effort

_____ 3. Show fairness in dealing with students

_____ 4. Attempt to resolve conflicts on the playground and in the classroom

_____ 5. Comply with requests without additional reminding

_____ 6. Change where necessary to adapt to new and different circumstances

_____ 7. Am punctual in arrival, turning in reports and assignments, and in meeting commitments

_____ 8. Have a minimum of distracting and irritating mannerisms

_____ 9. Am aware of teacher's needs and problems and seek opportunities to give assistance

_____ 10. Accept helpful suggestions

_____ 11. Follow instructions and directions

_____ 12. Show respect for rights, feelings, and opinions of others

_____ 13. Avoid judging students by adult standards

_____ 14. Encourage students to work with a spirit of cooperation

_____ 15. Am aware of students' interests

_____ 16. Attempt to give equal opportunities and equal attention to all students

_____ 17. Am mindful of individual differences, abilities, and needs

_____ 18. Help students use class time effectively

_____ 19. Make sufficient preparation for assigned responsibilities

_____ 20. Show sympathetic, understanding attitude toward children with problems

_____ 21. Am willing to admit errors or lack of knowledge about a particular area

_____ 22. Interact positively with the students

_____ 23. Take charge of one group of students while the teacher is working with another group

Sample II *(continued)*

_____ 24. Contribute daily to planning and long-range programs for the students

_____ 25. Participate in school activities

_____ 26. Participate in appropriate community activities

_____ 27. Am appropriately dressed for assigned duties

_____ 28. Use discretion when speaking of school or colleagues

_____ 29. Show a willingness to share ideas and techniques

_____ 30. Contribute constructively to committee work

_____ 31. Assist students in learning proper social habits, including being polite to others

_____ 32. Assist students in library work

_____ 33. Help students learn proper use of tools and equipment

_____ 34. Follow proper channels in making suggestions and initiating activities

_____ 35. Show resourcefulness in helping provide enrichment experiences for students

_____ 36. Help to keep the classroom neat and attractive

_____ 37. Use acceptable English in a clear and pleasant voice

_____ 38. Have good physical health

_____ 39. Show evidence of professional growth

Sample III

TEACHER AIDE SELF-EVALUATION CHECKLIST

Teacher Aide's Name_____ Date_____

School_____ Teacher's Name_____

Directions: Check the appropriate column

	Items	Always	Usually	Rarely
1.	Do I cooperate with the classroom teacher?			
2.	Do I exhibit initiative?			
3.	Do I follow through with lessons initiated by the teacher?			
4.	Am I dependable and reliable?			
5.	Do I check my completed assignments for mistakes and errors?			
6.	Am I aware of the importance of the responsibilities assigned?			
7.	Am I prompt in carrying out the duties assigned to me?			
8.	Do I follow closely the directions given by the teacher?			

Items	Always	Usually	Rarely
9. Do I plan for the activity that I have been assigned?			
10. Do I exhibit self-control?			
11. Are my dress and appearance appropriate?			
12. Do I listen to the children?			
13. Do I show evidence of professional growth?			
14. Do I follow proper channels in making suggestions and initiating activities?			
15. Do I enjoy my work?			
16. Do I treat children fairly?			
17. Am I able to secure the cooperation of the students?			
18. Am I courteous at all times?			
19. Do I present a favorable image of the school to the public?			

Items	Always	Usually	Rarely
20. Do I evaluate myself at regular intervals?			
21. Do I try to develop a friendly attitude toward all of my co-workers?			
22. Do I operate audiovisual equipment efficiently?			
23. Do children respond positively to me?			
24. Do children voluntarily come to me for advice?			
25. Am I conscious of each student's potential and needs?			
26. Am I trying to improve my speech patterns?			
27. Do I avoid criticism of the children, the teacher, and the school?			
28. Is my handwriting, both manuscript and cursive, improving?			
29. Do I strive to do my best at all times and take advantage of every opportunity to improve?			
30. Do I accept constructive criticism gracefully?			

your performance.

Accepting criticism is not a problem in itself, but how you handle it can be a problem. Every worker should expect to be criticized at some point and therefore should not consider criticism as a personal attack but as a suggestion for improvement of performance. You probably have already had some experience in handling various kinds of criticism in school or on another job. Yet, taking criticism gracefully from a teacher with whom you work every day can be a difficult matter.

Criticism is less difficult to handle if you consider it not as total rejection but only as a rejection of certain behavior patterns. When you accepted your first job as a teacher aide, it is unlikely that you received much formal training. Even if you had an internship, it was probably limited in time and quality. From a practical standpoint the old adage, "Experience is the best teacher," is true. Look upon your actual work experience as a continual learning opportunity. By thinking in this context, you will find it easier to accept suggestions and criticism without taking the criticism personally.

In addition, when you accept constructive criticism, that suggests that you do profit from your mistakes. Making mistakes is normal — human beings are not perfect — but to continue making the same mistakes repeatedly indicates that you have a serious problem. During the first few weeks on the job as a teacher aide, you are more likely to make mistakes because it takes time to learn routines and procedures. Likewise, you will need time to learn that teacher expectations differ from classroom to classroom. The first month or so, then, is a period when you can anticipate being corrected quite frequently. If you take time during the beginning months of your job to evaluate and to analyze your strengths and weaknesses, you can easily anticipate areas in which you need improvement. By examining some of your behavior traits that are criticized, you will be aware of the kinds of mistakes to avoid in the future.

For example, promptness is usually mentioned as a characteristic essential for getting along with others. If promptness has not been part of your life-style, you may have to be criticized several times before you feel motivated to change your behavior pattern. Being late may not be due to deliberate thoughtlessness on your part, but it will usually be interpreted by others as a "don't-care attitude." This kind of attitude irritates and alienates the classroom teacher. Promptness is particularly important if you are assuming a supportive role and people are depending on you to be in your area of responsibility at a certain time. The teacher may get tired of reminding you constantly of your tardiness and may choose instead to ask her administrator to assign a new aide to her classroom. There are few, if any, job assignments where promptness is not an important factor in evaluating job performance.

SUMMARY

Evaluation cannot achieve its intended purpose unless it is cooperatively approached by both the teacher and the aide. If the evaluation process is incorrectly handled, it can severely damage staff morale. The cooperative planning of a beneficial evaluation program offers valuable opportunities for better mutual understanding and stronger relationships.

Deciding who ultimately should evaluate a teacher aide depends on the needs of the particular school, as well as the overall abilities of its staff. Successful aide-evaluation programs can be found in which the principal, a supervisor, the classroom teacher, or the aides themselves do the evaluation. However, teacher aides, particularly those aspiring to enhance their own professional status, regard self-evaluation as the most acceptable method for evaluating performance.

SELECTED READINGS

Alexander, Kern. "What Teacher Aides Can — and Cannot — Do," *Nation's Schools*, Vol. 83, 23-25, August, 1968.

Blessing, Kenneth R. "Use of Teacher Aides in Special Education: A Review and Possible Application," *Exceptional Children*, Vol. 34, 107-113, October, 1967.

Bowman, Garda W. and Klopf, Gordon J. *New Partners in the Educational Enterprise*. New York: Bank Street College of Education, 1967.

Branan, Karen. "The Teacher Aide," *Parents' Magazine*, September, 1968.

Clough, Dick B. and Clough, Bonnie M. *Utilizing Teacher Aides in the Classroom*. Springfield, Ill.: Charles C Thomas, Publisher, 1978.

Cronin, Joseph M. "What's All This About Teacher Aides?" *California Journal of Secondary Education*, Vol. 34, 390-397, November, 1959.

DeLara, L. E. "Aides in the Junior High School," *The Clearing House*, Vol. 42, 234-237, December, 1967.

Denemark, George W. "The Teacher and His Staff," *Today's Education*, Vol. 55, 17-19, December, 1966.

DeVita, Joseph C. "A Day in the Life of a Teacher Aide," *Audio-Visual Instruction*, 152, May, 1968.

Esbensen, Thorwald. "Should Teacher Aides Be More Than Clerks?" *Phi Delta Kappan*, Vol. 47, 237, January, 1966.

Garvey, James F. *Handbook for Paraprofessionals*. Swarthmore, Pa.: Croft, Inc., 1968.

Harding, Alice Currie. "How Teacher Aides Feel About Their Jobs," *NEA Journal*, Vol. 56, 17-19, November, 1967.

Herman, Wayne L. "Teacher Aides: How They Can Be of Real Help," *Grade Teacher*, Vol. 84, 102-104, February, 1967.

National Education Association. *Auxiliary School Personnel*. Washington, D.C.: National Education Association, 1967.

Noar, Gertrude. *Teacher Aides at Work*. Washington, D.C.: National Educational Association, 1967.

Perkins, Bryce. *Getting Better Results from Substitutes, Teacher Aides, and Volunteers*. Englewood Cliffs, N.J.: Prentice-Hall, Inc., 1966.

Quill, Jeanne. *One Giant Step: A Guide for Head Start Aides*. Washington, D.C.: National Association for the Education of Young Children, 1968.

Robb, Mel H. *Teacher Assistants*. Columbus, Ohio: Charles E. Merrill Publishing Co., 1969.

Sunderlin, Sylvia (ed.). *Aides to Teachers and Children*. Washington, D.C.:

Association for Childhood Education International, 1967.
Utah State Board of Education. *Educational Aides.* Salt Lake City, Utah: Utah State Board of Education, 1973.
Wright, Betty A. *Teacher Aides to the Rescue.* New York: John Day, 1969.

INDEX

187